911 from your soul

911 from your soul

JEANINE THOMPSON

WORLDCHANGERS
MEDIA

Hardcover ISBN: 978-1-955811-21-7
Paperback ISBN: 978-1-955811-22-4
E-book ISBN: 978-1-955811-25-5
LCCN: 2022907601

First hardcover edition: June 2022

Cover photo by Shari Fleming Photography
Design & Typesetting by Bryna Haynes

Published by WorldChangers Media
PO Box 83, Foster, RI 02825
www.WorldChangers.Media

Dedication

To Tanner and Taylor:
You have been my greatest teachers, and my
daily inspiration to live my highest expression.
I love you beyond measure.

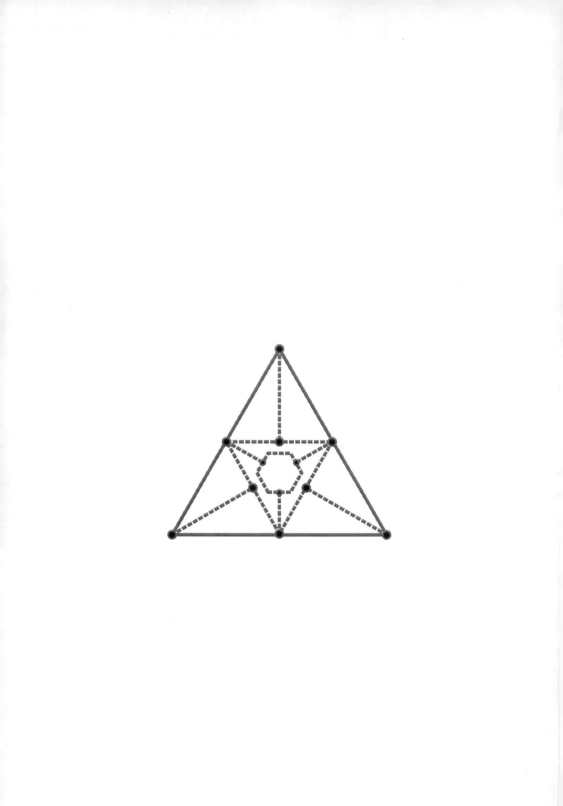

Praise

"In *911 From Your Soul*, Jeanine Thompson strikes a thoughtful balance between navigating our human experience in all its various iterations and exploring the vast field of potential available to all of us."

**– Dr. Sue Morter, bestselling author of *The Energy Codes*,
creator of BodyAwake® Yoga**

"Jeanine Thompson understands how to ignite and leverage the power of Soul and quantum potential for personal transformation—and, in turn, contribute greater business impact. This book is a must-read for any executive or high achiever who feels like conventional methods are no longer empowering them to access their full potential."

**– Steve Farber, founder of the Extreme Leadership Institute and
bestselling author of *Love Is Just Damn Good Business***

"If life is sending you challenges, there is no better way to meet them than to tap your own vast inner wisdom. In *911 From Your Soul*, Jeanine Thompson lays out a powerful and pragmatic pathway to create harmony between your inner world and your outer experience. Highly recommended!"

**– Jack Canfield, coauthor of the *New York Times* bestselling *Chicken Soup
for the Soul*® series, America's #1 Success Coach,
and author of *The Success Principles*™**

"This is a very personal, courageous book that shares Jeanine's story and how she found her own path and helps others find theirs. Everyone is searching for meaning, it is central to the journey of the human experience. However you source your answers, this read causes you to deeply reflect, discern your own truths, and be inspired to be of highest service to life."

– **Brad Anderson, former Chief Executive Officer, Best Buy**

"Jeanine's words and wisdom carry transformative energy that help people live their best lives. These expansive and practical methods to achieve mind/body/soul harmony gave me a new perspective on living a balanced and intentional life. An inspiring and essential read."

– **Philip Noyed, Top 60 Master Artist**

"Jeanine's The Soul Solution principles have the power to help you change your life, redefine your relationship to success, and live with more freedom and joy than you understood was possible. Highly recommended."

– **Heather Dawe, award-winning real estate agent**

"Liberating and brilliant! *911 From Your Soul* is a must-read that illuminates the solution to the unspoken longing within so many around the globe right now. Our Souls are calling us forward and Jeanine is a contemporary messenger for a lost and ancient truth. Trusted, grounded, and wise beyond convention, she will walk you home. A 'matchmaker for the Soul,' Jeanine is an intermediary for the sacred within and all around us."

– **Sara Jessica Laamanen, numerologist, performance consultant**

"Many of us are seeking answers in our lives. We're here without a definitive roadmap, but with a longing to live our best life. *911 From Your Soul* is a light on your path, providing tangible techniques and timeless guidance. This is a relatable read that offers inspiring new perspectives we all can benefit from."

– **Susan Marcinelli, PhD, former Fortune 50 SVP, advisor to CEOs and senior executives, author, and speaker**

"Wow! This book contains the messages I only wish I would have read twenty-plus years ago. As I read, my heart was warmed and pained, and many visualizations came to me on situations where I could have politely stood up and walked into a new life. And, the beauty is, we all still have time to do just that. Whether you are a global senior executive, a parent, or a child like my little son, this book has the wisdom messages you need to read, digest, absorb, and take action around in order to align to your most precious being ... you! A must-read for lifting of all our potentials."

Julie Gilbert, Partner, McKinsey & Company, Explosive Global Growth CEO, digital business builder

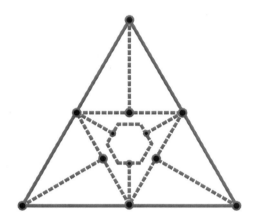

Contents

Foreword

by Marci Shimoff

I've never encountered anyone quite like Jeanine Thompson. With equal footing in the often-disparate worlds of spiritual consciousness and business, Jeanine manages to rise effortlessly into the upper reaches of both. The first time we met, on a Zoom interview for *Your Miraculous Life* program in which I personally mentor eight women, I remember thinking, "This is someone who is truly on fire to do powerful work in the world."

About halfway through that program, our group came together for a three-day retreat in Northern California. We sat to begin the day's meditation, a circle of inspiring humans surrounded by a circle of majestic redwood trees, and within moments, my whole body was covered with goosebumps—what I call "god-bumps."

Something important is happening, I thought.

Then, I looked at Jeanine. Light shone down upon her and radiated around her. Tears streamed down her face. In that moment, it was clear something was awakening within her.

Later, I found out from Jeanine that our meditation had birthed a new expression of the work she was called to do with conscious high performers and business leaders. The idea for "Soul 911" had come through for her in those moments—and the seeds had been planted for what would eventually become this brilliant work.

I feel honored and humbled that this beautiful book was, in some part, birthed in our midst. In fact, the experiences Jeanine had on our retreat—like getting in touch with the wisdom of the trees, the potency of Nature, and the guidance available from the Soul—are all themes you'll encounter in these pages. Higher guidance and the Soul's wisdom is always available. It's simply up to us to listen to these messages and share them for the highest good of all.

You may be tempted, after reading this recollection, to think, "Oh, this is another one of those 'woo-woo' spiritual books." You'd be mistaken. Jeanine's work is Soul-inspired and Soul-directed, and it's also pragmatic and practical. This is where the rubber meets the road in terms of human consciousness—the space where infinite understanding meets action, and spiritual principles meet success metrics. This work is, in essence, a new paradigm for success on both a personal and collective level, one that is supportive of the full brilliance of *you*.

In my career, I've spent a lot of time training individuals

and groups within Fortune 100 companies, particularly in the areas of happiness and self-management. Over and over again, I've witnessed brilliant, passionate people chasing success and achievement because they believe it will bring them happiness—and over and over again, happiness becomes the price of that achievement. It is possible to have both success *and* fulfillment; achievement *and* inner well-being. In fact, it's more than possible; it's vital for humanity's evolution.

Aristotle said, "Happiness is the meaning and purpose of life, the whole aim and end of human existence." But happiness is an inside job. In fact, I would assert that it is our *only* job—because in the pursuit of happiness, we must meet ourselves, and discover what has been hidden within us all along. Authentic and lasting happiness is the highest expression of consciousness.

Since I was featured in Rhonda Byrne's film *The Secret* in 2006, the world has changed dramatically. Information that was once considered esoteric has become commonplace. Meditation and gratitude practices are now ubiquitous among high performers. We, as a society, have been awakening. It's beautiful, powerful, and inspiring.

However, the time has come to move beyond mere awakening. Now, we need to do the work of living into what we have learned.

Jeanine's work is pivotal to this evolution. Her Soul Solution method is among the most effective I've encountered for empowering people to master key spiritual principles in daily living. In her dynamic exploration of Earth View, Soul View, and the harmonious ground between them, you will discover

Soul's presence in all aspects of your life, even when—especially when—it all seems to be falling apart.

The focus of this book is on the individual and the interior journey. Transformation must occur within before it can be leveraged outwardly to facilitate a greater good. And while the emphasis in this book is spiritual, it's fully grounded by Jeanine's breadth of professional knowledge and experience, which spans multiple disciplines and professional expressions. Her work is truly a bridge needed to navigate the challenges and crucial questions that all of us, in one way or another, are currently facing. While you'll do the work in this book on your own (although not alone, as you'll learn), its gifts will permeate every aspect of your life.

In essence, this book is a roadmap to a different kind of success—the kind that comes when you're aligned with the truth of who you are and you live your life accordingly. The kind of success that flows when you deeply understand that life is always on your side. The kind that allows you to be fully present for what matters, while at the same time creating a more loving and exciting future.

Creating success in this way allows you to experience happiness, health, fulfillment, and purpose. More, it allows you to harness the power of love, and become a true change agent in your own life and the lives of others.

*** Marci Shimoff***

#1 *New York Times* bestselling author of *Happy for No Reason*
and *Chicken Soup for the Woman's Soul*

Introduction

I find the universe quite clever.

If you had told me thirty years ago, when I was practicing evidence-based psychotherapy, that I would write a book like this one, I would have laughed out loud. If it wasn't a "proven" protocol, it wasn't even on my radar.

Eighteen years ago, although I was starting to question what I thought I knew (and had, in fact, embarked on a search I was not yet aware of), I would have dismissed the notion of this work immediately, and in the next breath moved on to juggling my overfull agenda.

However, that was before I heard the 911 from my Soul—before life spoke in a voice I couldn't ignore, and sent me on a wonderful, topsy-turvy, completely unanticipated journey home to myself, and to the greater truth of who I am becoming.

Something quite beautiful happens when life as we know it falls apart—when the knowledge, skills, and abilities that previously served us work less effectively, or not at all. Suddenly, we become more open to exploring other ways of thinking. Wisdom bits and solutions that were not available to us in our previous states appear to show us the way and guide us to expansive new answers.

If you read the title of this book and thought, "This is for me!" (or if you thought, "I'm not sure this is for me," and picked it up anyway), chances are a new way of understanding and moving through life is beckoning. Maybe you feel like things are collapsing around you, and you don't know how to make sense of it all. Maybe you've undergone (or are in the midst of) a major life transformation and are looking for perspective and a way forward. Or maybe you simply feel like something is missing in your life—something beyond wealth, status, or the material goods we're trained to desire.

Either way, life is speaking.

Quietly or loudly, subtly alluding or unmistakably insisting that you wake up to that something stirring, life is inviting you to embark on a quest. Not the kind that will take you to a far-away landscape where your current life seems only a dream, but one that will take you deeper into yourself. This path is exquisitely beautiful and at times quite challenging. In the inner-scape, a terrain like none other awaits—one that will invariably change your life for the better. Only there can you discern your truths, release conditioned habits and roles that no longer serve you, and come home to the only real home there is: your Soul.

Yes. *That* is the call you are hearing. You are being called to return to Soul, and to the fullest potentiality of who you are.

Many are hearing this call right now. Like the historical period which we now call the Renaissance (the literal word meaning rebirth or reawakening), this call is coming on the heels of a time of upheaval and crisis—namely, the ongoing global pandemic which began in 2020 and which continues through the time of this writing.

Most of my clients are senior executives, leaders, and entrepreneurs who are high performers. They've excelled and succeeded on many levels in life and business. They are smart, talented, and dedicated. However, they feel that something pivotal is missing from their very full, even enviable lives. They seek me out because they sense there is more that exists *beyond* their success. Even those who seek coaching to advance the next level of their personal potential do so within a broader context of desired life experiences. They perceive that a greater possibility exists for them, and feel a compelling urge to figure out why their go-to strategies aren't providing the answers they seek.

Before we meet, many potential clients think I'm going to offer an upgraded version of the same coaching they're used to. After all, I'm a former Fortune 50 executive, a Certified High-Performance Coach (CHPC), a former licensed psychotherapist who specialized in leading-edge treatment of anxiety disorders, and a Rapid Transformational Therapy Practitioner (RTTP). These are a few of the credentials, knowledge sets, and methodologies I draw upon steeped in science, proven methods, and grounded in real-world business.

Yet I'm also a certified Reiki Master and former Registered Yoga Teacher (RYT-200). I work extensively with energy, meditation, spiritual, and heart-based practices. I work in the proven and the felt, the seen and the unseen.

When my clients' reliance on what created their past success is no longer enough, I invite them to take the one journey they have not yet pursued: a journey into themselves. Only there can they find the meaning, peace, joy, and aliveness they truly desire.

Perhaps you are in a similar position. Whether life is speaking loudly or quietly, through heartbreak or restlessness or somewhere in between, you are being called home to yourself by a 911 from your Soul.

How *To* Use This Book

This book contains seven core spiritual principles—The Soul Solution—that will guide you along your journey home to yourself. These are informed by my own path and learnings, as well as timeless wisdom and modern science. I love the "and" inherent in this structure: it is a fusion of soul and science, the invisible and the visible, the etheric and the tangible. While there will always remain great mysteries in life—areas where none of us can ever "know" for sure—there is a space into which we can move that is *real*, but not yet proven. That is the place I am inviting you into.

We are in that "test and try" phase with the sciences of consciousness and energy. Cutting-edge research is starting to prove that it's real—that we are more than just a collection of organs and electrical impulses, and that the brain isn't the sole source of our consciousness and identity. Yet, we are still building the knowledge base upon which the later phases of the scientific process will be grounded.

More, this work is intended to invite you to reexplore and challenge what you "know" about each of these principles and present a new Soul View of each to contrast with the Earth View of our current understanding. Consciousness, as science is proving, operates at a different level than human knowledge, emotion, and thought. We, as humans, have access to a literal universe of information beyond what our five senses can perceive—and it is this perspective that will guide us in creating real change, purpose, connection, and joy in our lives.

It's my intention that, by the time you finish this book, you will have the tools to navigate your personal 911 from your Soul, and also to see the interconnectedness of every inflection point of your life to a greater, intelligent whole. Whatever is unfolding for you, this book is intended to guide you to discern the truths of all that life is offering to you, and through you.

More than anything, this book is intended to be felt and experienced. Despite its sometimes "ethereal" subject matter, it's not theoretical; rather, it's explorational. It is an invitation to sit with your Soul, wrestle with the big questions in your life, and open the door to tangibly living your fullest potentiality. You'll be asked to navigate and dance with paradox: the seen and the unseen, the felt and the perceived, the proven and the not-yet-proven.

So, I invite you to read with an open heart. The rational, logical mind will bump you up against your tendencies to desire mastery and success; that dynamic won't fully serve you here. Often, great truths precede collective acceptance—and in this book, you are being invited to walk that edge for your own growth and expansion. Some of the practices I offer are likely to feel practical, tangible, and "just make sense." Others will feel out of your comfort zone, or just plain "out there."

Test and try. See what happens. And above all, remember you are wired for this.

My intention is that this work offers you an expanded yet grounded way of moving through life as the highest expression of your true nature. May you feel empowered and inspired to leverage what you learn in these pages to find your own answers, discern your own truths, and clarify your next right actions. Untapped wisdom and universal intelligence already exist within you and all around you; when you embrace it through these Seven Principles, the way you see, engage with, and experience life will be radically transformed for the better.

Your Soul is speaking.

You are more than you know yourself to be.

You are limitless, infinite, and whole.

You are ready.

Welcome.

Part I

The Call

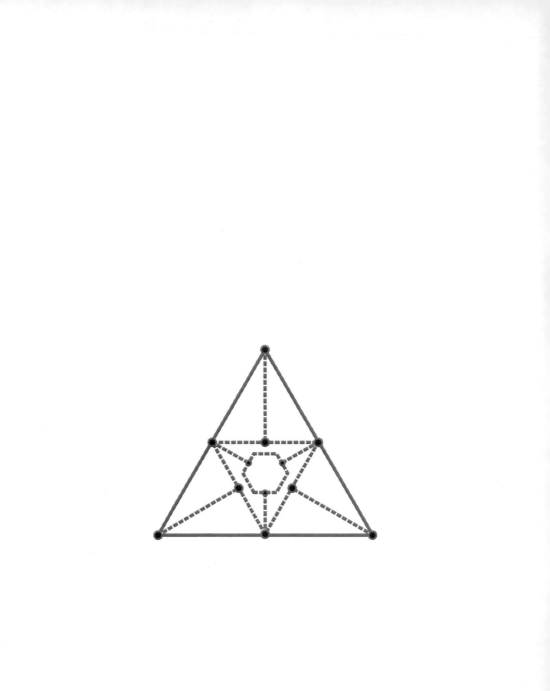

Chapter 1

Turning Point

It was a typical day in my life as an international executive. I woke up excited, and within minutes was wildly tossing clothes and toiletries into my suitcase to prepare for my flight home from Shanghai, China. (As my fellow travel warriors know, repacking to go home never seems to matter as much. It's like, "Shove the stuff in and let's do this!")

I checked the drawers, floors, and closet of my hotel room. Arranged my driver and transport. Checked out of the hotel, nodding at the bright-eyed, cheerful front desk manager. Locked in the backup plan with my friend just in case my flight was delayed; if she didn't hear from me, she would pick up my kids at school. Soon, I was hearing the familiar greeting over the airport loudspeakers: "Welcome to Shanghai!"

And home I flew.

I had made this trip, and others like it, many times before. It usually went something like this. Catch a flight early on Monday morning. Arrive very, *very* early on Tuesday morning. Work my tail off on Tuesday, Wednesday, and Thursday. Survive on coffee, belief in the mission, and love for my team. Hop on the plane Friday morning, and—a mere twelve hours later—touch down on the tarmac in Minneapolis. Spend the weekend ecstatic to see my kids and sleep in my own bed. Rinse and repeat. Different country. Same drill.

But this time was different.

Not at first. I boarded the plane without issue. Takeoff was right on time. It was all very well-planned and executed. I took a deep breath and prepared to relax until the next leg of the process.

I often used my flight time to reflect on how blessed I was. Yes, it was stressful and demanding to be holding a high-level leadership position as a single mom; it was also fun, rewarding, and exhilarating. I loved my wise, amazing kids. I loved the company, my CEO, and the senior team I worked with. I loved all the employees who worked with and for me and who were part of creating our company's enormous success. I loved the excitement and adventure of traveling and learning so much about and from all of the employees and customers we served around the globe.

I landed in Minneapolis early that afternoon, a bit ragged yet excited to be home. Of course, the first thing I did after grabbing my luggage was check my phone for emails and calls. A most atypical message awaited me. I'd been called in to corporate headquarters immediately. It appeared my friend would have to pick up my kids after all.

While I was away, the company I worked for had developed a cost-cutting strategy that included a very generous voluntary buy-out package that would be offered to nearly all of the 4,000 corporate employees.

This was *so* not part of my carefully-curated life plan.

What in the world are they doing? I wondered, as I left the office later that day. *This is absolutely crazy. Offering a buy-out option to the top talent could ravage the organization.*

I had fourteen days to make a decision. I could maintain the status quo, and even reach for another promotion. Or, I could take the severance package and step into the unknown.

At first, I had no intention of leaving. It wasn't the right time; in fact, it was about four years ahead of my plan. Nevertheless, as it became increasingly clear that the senior team I adored would likely all be leaving, I was left to wonder: would I still love my job if many of the people who made it great were gone?

Each night, I papered my floors with lists of pros and cons, benefits and risks. I could keep my sixty-hour work weeks, continue flying 200,000-plus international miles each year, and continue climbing the ladder at a world-leading consumer electronics retailer. I could maintain my daily hustle, with a calendar so packed that my women colleagues would sometimes follow the click of my stiletto heels into the restroom to squeeze in a few extra minutes of meeting time. Or, I could face my fear of leaping without the cushy, corporate safety net, and begin to envision a life that was … my own. But, beyond vague thoughts of starting a coaching business, I didn't have the slightest idea what I wanted to do, or where I might end up.

The voices of all the "experts" I'd consulted with looped in my mind, cautioning that exiting now was ill-advised—a risky financial decision that could undercut my earning potential for the rest of my life. Growing up in a small Minnesota farming community on reduced lunches and hand-me-down clothes, I had seen corporate success as my pathway out of a life that felt insecure and fraught with stress. I was always loved and cared for, yet I had sworn long ago that I would never be that poor again—that I would avoid poverty *at all costs*. And here I was, considering a move that might literally kill the security I'd labored so diligently to build.

For many of my peers, the decision to leave was a no-brainer. They would just bank the cash and move on to the next big gig. However, most of them had a very different setup than I did. They had more financial cushion, more stability, and family to help manage the craziness of life on the road. Still, even in my confusion, I knew I wasn't deciding between staying put and making a parallel move. If I left, I sensed it would be a permanent path.

I cried myself to sleep each night, sometimes collapsing right on top of my growing piles of "pros and cons" lists. But every morning, I put my brave face back on, and was the embodiment of calm for my children and coworkers. It was, I was realizing, a role I played well. Maybe *too* well.

Then, I remembered a moment that had happened six months

prior. While on vacation in Mexico, I'd suddenly blurted, "I can't do this forever. It's time for a change when the kids graduate." It was like something—or someone—else was speaking through me. I just about dropped my cocktail on the floor.

Suddenly, that same voice was present within me again. I could feel it, hear it, calling me magnetically toward a path that was not yet defined. It was simultaneously terrifying and exciting.

In the night, I would lay awake and hear it speaking to me. *You literally run from one demand to another. You are never present for anything, even when you are physically there. Your mind is always consumed with the next call, the next meeting, the next trip. You don't even smell the fresh-cut grass anymore. You feel guilty when you're not with your kids, and guilty when you're not at work.*

You are not really living.

When I allowed myself to dance with this honesty, I felt it: the nagging restlessness, the persistent yearning for "something more." It had been with me for years. While I was great at keeping up the façade, the truth was that the things I had previously loved—the team, the mission, the challenge, the accoutrements of success—these no longer inspired me as they once had. I was tired of trying to look perfect, be perfect, be more, know more, do more, and for heaven's sake keep everything *under control!*

These were not new feelings. What kept tripping me up was the fact that there was *nothing wrong* with my life. I liked being able to provide for my family. I liked my generous salary and the benefits it afforded us. I liked having the freedom to do what I wanted. I liked constantly being challenged to learn and grow. Still, as many times as my rational mind screamed, "For fuck's sake, stay put and be grateful!" that subtler, wiser part of me whispered, "There's more for you—and *through* you."

And somehow, by grace, I managed to listen.

I took the package. And stepped into my next calling.

Redefining "Potential"

To live at our highest potential is to be fully alive and fully expressed.

But what does that actually mean?

We've been taught that "potential" means attaining maximum hustle, success, money, and power. There is nothing wrong with any of those things; they can be beautiful, when created with integrity and in unity with your greater life. Yet there's another side to potential that lives in that most brilliant (and sometimes less obvious) place of *harmony.*

More and more, I work with clients who are longing to exist in the "and." Family/friends *and* career. Business *and* spirituality. Intellect *and* intuition. Work *and* play. Making a difference *and* having the lifestyle experiences they desire. Excellence *and* ease. They want to experience harmony with all that matters most to them: family, career, treasured relationships, joy, health, prosperity, connection, freedom, impact, fulfillment, and love.

Living in one polarity, many people I work with express that something is missing, yet they can't seem to put their finger on what it is. There's only the feeling that if they don't crack the code on this restlessness and yearning, they will not have lived their best life, or achieved their personal definition of success—and they will, in the end, regret it.

Sometimes, a signal that you're not living into your highest potential or greatest possibility is clear. You can see it in the relationship that's no longer fulfilling, mutually beneficial, or even salvageable; in the job that no longer gives you the same juice; in the body that you've neglected in the name of achievement and is now speaking to you in the language of pain or disease.

Other times, it's more subtle. It's there in your tight shoulders, your sleepless nights, your short fuse, or your growing anxiety. It's in the moments where you want to be somewhere else, doing what you value most, but work is unrelenting. (Projects need to be delivered, after all, and those you love will understand, it's just this once …)

It's not always evident at first why the restlessness and yearning are there. Nevertheless, over time—and it *will* happen, every single time—the whispers you hear in those quiet moments will get louder. The feelings will get stronger. And at some point, you won't be able to turn the dial down anymore.

"What the heck is going on?" you'll ask yourself. Because, from the outside, your life might look pretty darn great. You tell yourself you've worked hard to get here; you should be happy, or at least satisfied. Yet, you aren't—and deep down, you know it.

You're in search of the "and."

There's a way for you to show up in your life—a way for you to live, work, and play—that brings you to that intersection. To a place where everything you value is present, and nothing is missing—a place where you can finally be at peace, and where your yearning can be transmuted, fulfilled, and satiated.

Will you listen? Will you hear those 3:00 a.m. whispers, that quiet voice? Will you make the choice to go where you're being called?

I've been a hospice volunteer since graduate school, both formally and informally. Often, as I sit with people whose physical lives are ending, they speak about the years flying by in the blink of an eye. Nearly all of them thought they had more time. More time to enjoy life and do all of the things they had put off until a better time. More time to make a different choice. More time to have that difficult conversation. More time to be the person they knew they could become. And then—*bam!* Life shifted, and suddenly they were living their last days or months in this round of Earth School. They spoke with such clarity and conviction about what really mattered—connection, relationships, love—and what, in retrospect, did not matter at all.

The lesson from these beautiful souls is clear: if you want a life with no regrets, seize the precious, gifted moments *now*. Peace and joy are enlivened by the deep knowing that you gave it your all, and left nothing on the table.

So, if you are feeling the pull ...

If you are hearing the whisper ...

If you are at a critical point of choice in your life, and you're being called forward into the unknown …

You are not alone.

Countless others are on the same journey.

If you've ignored signals, told yourself you'd "get to it later," or allowed the voices of reason and safety to drown out the invitation, now is the time. Now is *your* time.

You picked up this book for a reason. Something resonated. Maybe it's because what you're hearing, feeling, and sensing is a 911 from your Soul. Maybe what you'll experience will be instrumental in realizing more of your true nature. Or, maybe you'll become a lighthouse for another.

What I trust is this: of all the things you could be doing or the places you could be right now, you are *here*. There is something of value for you in these pages. Some gift awaits you.

Welcome.

Hearing *the* Call

Sometimes, there are no trails of clues leading to your 911—no way you could have seen it coming. Some calls arrive unexpected, and undesired. Sudden loss, extreme tragedies, terminal illness, natural disasters, the death of a loved one, or a deep heartbreak will often prompt people to ask, "What else is there? What is life really about?"

If that's where you are, I surround you in love. May you receive all the guidance, love, and assistance you deserve and need. This book will support you as you navigate your journey—and, at the same time, it is *not* a substitute for trauma-informed professional help that can provide you with more immersive support and services. If the pain is raw and you are struggling day to day, I encourage the route of professional support first. Then, when the time is right, come back to this book and begin again.

When you listen to people who have pursued radical paths of love, fulfillment, and impact, you'll hear story after story of the powerful, painful catalysts that pulled them forward onto their new path. When life brought them to the point of surrender, they heard the voice of their Soul loud and clear, and answered the call. Remarkably they go on to become a beacon of light, hope, and inspiration to others. They endured unimaginable pain; and yet, because of what they lived through and how they now live beyond it, they have become our teachers about love and life.

No matter what you are living through right now—even if it feels insurmountable—there is something blessed on the other side.

For many of us, though, the call is more subtle. It finds us at the crossroads, in the place of choice. The yearning, restlessness, dissatisfaction, and fear of regret are an invitation to step away from the path we are traveling and take a new road—one that will return us to our essential nature.

Life is a spiritual journey. Every breath, every relationship, every joy and sorrow are calling you to remember who you really are, and to be and experience all that you came here for. Our discomforts, challenges, and even crises are invitations to free ourselves, expand our wings and rise into our highest expression—for ourselves, for those we love, and for all of humanity.

"Wow," you may be thinking. "We've wandered a long way from 'corporate exec taking a severance package.'"

Actually, we haven't.

That message when I got off the plane from Shanghai was the seeding of a call from my Soul—and the choice to follow it has changed my life in ways I never could have anticipated.

In hindsight, my Soul had been reaching out to me for a long time. There was that moment in Mexico. There were the nights when I lay awake, wracked with guilt about being away from my kids all week, every week—whether physically across the globe, or while at home with my energy scattered between competing demands. I struggled mightily to balance it all.

(Note: I'm not sure *balance* is possible. Harmony, however—that's the ticket!)

There were times I was so tired I could barely think, and instead of pausing to deeply listen, I chose to plaster on a smile and keep going. I made everything *okay*—or so I told myself. The 911 had to get louder before I could hear it for what it was.

Tune in and see if any of these are resonant for you.

- You feel lost and unsure about the trajectory of your life, and the traditional resources that served you in the past are no longer working.
- Things that used to bring you joy are falling flat.
- You feel a persistent yearning—like something is missing or off.

- You feel restlessness you can't seem to resolve.
- You run from opportunity to opportunity, looking for some trace of your old spark.
- You're spending more and more time rationalizing, denying, or distracting yourself in the hope that your inner discomfort will magically dissolve.
- You're being asked to radically change some aspect of your life (or, life seems to be forcing such a change on you), and some part of your familiar identity has been shaken or stripped away.
- Your life has been turned upside down. You're wondering how you will survive, and if joy will ever be possible again.
- You are hiding out or playing smaller than you know is possible for you.
- You fear living "out loud" as who you truly are.
- You are grappling with the bigger questions in life, such as, "What is the purpose of life? Who am I, and what am I here to do?"

The thing about a 911 is, it cannot be buttoned neatly into one simple statement or singular experience. Maybe you relate to one or more of the above statements, or maybe they don't quite explain how you're feeling or what you're going through. Although the above tend to be common warning flags, they may also be precursors to a 911, or your version of a full-on 911. Your experience will be unique to you. Maybe you're dealing with one clear issue, or maybe it's a series of accumulated experiences that feel overwhelming and become a 911.

For each of us, there will come a time when our Soul longs to birth something for us, and through us. Often this is the thing that we most strongly resist, are afraid of, or think we aren't ready for. When we ignore the call, it doesn't go away; it gets louder. Eventually, it becomes a 911.

My own 911 was quiet, in a way. I'd dealt with what seemed to be far bigger stressors in my life. While I was still in high school, I watched one of my best friends die. A coworker I admired lost her life soon after in a car accident. My two children were born with fairly severe medical challenges, and we navigated eight years of tough medical procedures and searing pain that, as a parent, I desperately wanted to fix and couldn't. All were hugely challenging and transformational.

It could have been my divorce. It could have been playing peacekeeper in my family as I took on the task of helping to support my dad financially and emotionally. It could have been the stress-related ulcerative colitis that, for years, required me to wear an adult diaper on long road trips to prevent mortifying embarrassment if we couldn't find a bathroom in time.

Yet my 911 was none of those things. *Why?*

Why did these life challenges not escalate into a 911? There is no doubt that each of those experiences were very painful. Each came with tons of tough nights, tears, and fears. They certainly shaped and changed how I walked through life in invaluable ways. They taught me compassion and wisdom. Yet I now suspect that, for me, they were not 911s because I simply wasn't open or ready yet to receive the call from my Soul. There is an unexplainable divine timing to our unfolding and what ignites the search for what is sacred that we cannot rush.

Before my 911, I was so steeped in, and aligned with, what was "proven"—research, logic, linear thinking—that the subtle language of my Soul could not be (or, more accurately, *was not*) heard or noticed. Layer on my strong resiliency and natural optimism, and lace in my hyper-focus on fixing, controlling, and moving back to sunshine and smiles as quickly as possible … well, you can see how I would have missed the cues.

We all undergo challenges in life. The distinction with a 911 is that there is a magnetic pull deep within ourselves, a luring forward, that accompanies the challenge. There is a bubbling-up of new questions that, try as you might, you can no longer brush over, sweep aside, or avoid. It might speak loudly; it might scream. Or, it might whisper subtly, yet with such persistence that you simply cannot ignore it.

Ultimately, it prompts a holy reassembly of who you are, and who you know yourself to be. Life is speaking, and it's asking you to grow beyond where you've been.

During a 911, you may wake up to everything you've been keeping yourself too busy to acknowledge, and all the ways you've been squeezing yourself into a box you didn't create or desire. All the parts of you seeking growth and evolution are calling for your attention. You may be directed to take action you don't understand or have feared. You may be invited to embody greater courage, truth, and alignment—to step, as I'll show you in this book, into the space of the "and," where all of you can be present and find room to thrive.

You've always been in search of this, whether you are aware of it or not. At the core of you is a deep, primal longing—a longing to meet yourself and live in union with the sacred, which is within, beyond, and all around you.

And yet, we miss or deny that call for months, even years. Why? Because it works for us not to address the struggle. We often prefer the pain of the familiar to the fear of the unknown. Humans can be extreme in our avoidance of change and loss. As long as life is still working (sort of), we see no reason to blow it all up. Why rock the boat that's still afloat?

I think we've lost sight. We've forgotten we are more than human beings that do and acquire and produce. We deeply crave love, beauty, awe, and wonder. We crave freedom and belonging. We crave to potentiate to our fullest nature. Still, we don't allow ourselves to actually go there.

When was the last time you let a sunset take your breath away, or really listened to the sound of the ocean waves as the salty air caressed your face? When was the last time you felt totally at peace, or connected to something bigger than yourself? When was the last time you felt true freedom? When was the last time you had a sacred experience, or knew that you *mattered*?

This is what your Soul is calling you home to.

You are *longing* for a path back to your sacred self.

If this book found you, chances are you are already a seeker. You've likely pursued myriad professional and personal development courses, seminars, and retreats. You probably devour books, podcasts, and audio trainings. You care about being your best— yet, despite your constant pursuit of growth, you sense that a greater possibility exists. Traditional best practices and resources that once served you exceptionally well are no longer sufficient, and you need a differentiated advantage and approach.

In other words, it's time to move from *seeking* to *seeing.*

This book is for you if you are ready to tune into the 911, explore why and how you are being called forward, and learn to move through life in a new way. If you are open to and curious about a range of perspectives—from science-based psychology, neurology, biology, physiology, and quantum research to spiritual and mystical perspectives and the deeper questions of life—you will find all of them here in this book.

However, if you are convinced that you're doing everything right and that life is just throwing you a curveball, or if exploring spiritual, metaphysical, and otherwise "invisible" aspects of life makes you roll your eyes, you may want to stop reading now. I promise, I won't be offended. (I did plenty of my own eye-rolling years ago. Remember, timing is everything.)

Soul Triage

In my practice with clients, there is often a divergent response when they learn what I've just shared with you. Some feel relieved and validated that others have also gone through what they're experiencing, and they are excited to dive in and learn more. Others share they are befuddled or reeling a bit. What they thought was garden-variety restlessness or discomfort has been revealed as something potentially far bigger and more transformational.

Wherever you are, let's pause and honor it. Grab a cup of tea, or a glass of water. Let yourself be still for a moment. If your brain is busy and your mind isn't silent, it's okay; just take a few deep breaths, and silently whisper, "I am open. I am listening." You don't have to figure it out today, or even next week. You don't have to know right now what it all means, or even who you are whispering to. For now, it's simply a signal to yourself and to the universe, that you are curious and listening.

As you continue through this book, you will find many exercises, journaling prompts, and other tangible practices to help you integrate the information you're learning. Do them! Experience is far more powerful and rewarding than reading alone. Keep a journal close by as you read. Allow answers to emerge from within you as you get more clarity. Capture what arises even if it doesn't make sense. If nothing is bubbling up initially, no worries. The commitment to experiment is most important at this point.

My intention is that, when you've completed this book, you will have come to know yourself more deeply. May you meet the "you" whom you've been longing to meet. May the practices and perspectives offered ignite your rediscovery and redefinition of your personal truths. May you experience invaluable insights and generative meanings around your life experiences thus far. May you be blown away by the utter brilliance of how life has moved to you, through you, and away from you in service to your deeper calling. May you be inspired to discover your true nature while sparking a more fulfilling way of being, living, and contributing.

Most of all, may aligning with your Soul lead to greater confidence and courage to take new actions, to live fully alive and out loud, with more joy and ease, with enhanced relationships that uplift fellow Earth travelers.

May you feel seen, supported, held, and loved, and remember that you never travel alone.

And, with that, let's begin.

Chapter 2

Reentry

W hat in the world did you just *do*, Thomps?"

This was the question I asked myself several days after jumping ship from corporate life. Lying in bed—having woken up to soft sunlight instead of a buzzing alarm and a barrage of emails and calls from the night before (because heaven forbid I sleep and miss something "urgent")—I struggled to wrap my mind around the scale of the change I'd just chosen. I still felt like it was all a dream.

For a person who prided herself in carefully curating her life, this limbo of uncertainty felt unsettling, at times terrifying, and completely irresponsible. I felt like I had just jumped off a bridge onto a net full of holes—a sketchy support that could give way without notice at any time.

Little did I know what life-enhancing growth would result

from my choice to undertake this journey. The seeds that had been planted would grow into unimaginably beautiful blooms.

This was the magical alchemy brewing up in the cauldron of my core. But on that long-ago morning, all I could think was, "Oh, *shit*."

We rarely talk about what happens in the immediate aftermath of a big leap. We talk about endings, and beginnings, but rarely that uncomfortable space in between. Yet in that space—which some teachers call "the fertile void"—something very important happens. We unwrite the scripts that have kept us locked in the same cycles for months, years, or even decades.

Of course I was freaking out. I had no plan, no answers. No map—at least, not one I was consciously aware of. I had only my choice, and the insatiable yearning and restlessness that was growing stronger by the day.

My mission became to figure out what was causing that uncomfortable feeling. In the past, I'd rushed to smooth over discomfort, polish up the rough spots, and keep moving along. *Problem. Gap. Hole. Fix it! Chop, chop. Get on with it, Punkin. This is life!*

I did the "moving along" and "finding the bright spots" really well—which was a gift, and also at times a serious impediment. My diverse list of skills and credentials now seemed rather useless. I wasn't too busy to pay attention to this feeling. I wasn't busy *at all.* Outside of my kids' school schedules, there was literally nothing I *had to* do. Worse, I had no idea how to *be* in this uncertain, messy, still, oh-so-quiet in-between space.

I'd heard the platitudes. *Live from the inside out. Be present. The only way out is in.* I suspected these ideas held something for me, yet I couldn't put my finger on what.

So, I did what I did best: I moved along. Only this time, I was on a mission to discover what this whole "in" thing was all about.

At first, I just played. And slept. (Turns out, cultivating a healthy and consistent sleep schedule after years of international time zone hopscotch is no easy feat!) It had also been years—okay, more like decades—since I *felt* free to play. I began to embrace and cherish the ordinary moments, like driving the kids to school and talking about whatever they wanted to, having leisurely lunches with friends, and fully listening to conversations around the dinner table. Holy wow … the ordinary really is *extra*ordinary. Before, I'd been a master at double-tasking: taking work calls as I drove the kids to school, answering emails as we watched TV at night, scheduling meetings while en route to other meetings. I prided myself on how many balls I could keep in the air at any given time. I wanted to be ever-available, particularly for my employees in opposite time zones—and I was. It was a badge of honor that served no one—and I was finally beginning to realize it.

Most of all, during this in-between time, I gave myself *permission*. Permission to lay around all day. Permission to do absolutely nothing that smacked of "productivity." Permission to take my time. Permission to focus on one thing at a time. Permission to actually enjoy my life.

It all felt so ironic. I thought for so long that my corporate career was my ticket to liberation. For years, I did my best to rationalize and ease the feelings of guilt when I was less present or available for family and friends. Those lost daily moments were sacrifices made on the altar of future freedom. *Someday,* I told myself, *this will all be worth it. For all of us.*

Yet, life doesn't happen at some point in an unknown future. It happens now. On this day. In this moment.

Beyond What *is* "Proven"

Best practices have been a game changer for me, both in healthcare and across diverse ecosystems of business. Drawing upon established knowledge and proven approaches, following Standard Operating Procedures (SOPs) and seeking out mentors with greater expertise were invaluable. Whether I was obtaining expert guidance on providing psychotherapy for trauma related to the horrific acts of a renowned serial killer, pursuing advanced training for evidence-based treatment of anxiety disorders, or making a big career leap from psychotherapy to business leadership; learning from esteemed teachers and wisdom was pivotal and priceless.

The clients I work with respect best practices and SOPs, too. They are high achievers hungry to know, integrate, and create with, and beyond, the best-known information. With aligned SOPs, individuals and companies can achieve efficiency, safety, a scalable and consistent brand experience, and many other benefits.

As vital and valuable as these practices are, they also have limitations. During the Covid-19 pandemic, we witnessed first-hand how existing standards and methods required significant adaptations to meet the unprecedented conditions—or how they failed to work at all. Even in less extreme conditions, we might operate from outdated information and procedures, either because we are too busy to change them, or we've gotten so comfortable with them that we are no longer open to cutting-edge information that might shift or shake up our beliefs or routines.

As I floundered in my "in-between," it rapidly became clear that my previous best practices were no longer sufficient to explain or deal with what was happening inside of me.

This wasn't due to any lack of effort or striving on my part. Rather, it was because commonly accepted and practiced standards at best dismissed—and at worst, entirely negated—the power of my inner knowing and my ability to draw upon the vast, invisible intelligence available to me. Rather than analyzing or creating solutions informed *solely* by objective and external vantage points, I was being called to a new way of sourcing and operating.

Couple that with the paradox of high achievers, who often push themselves in pursuit of the next achievement by relying upon more of the same knowledge, skills, practices, and abilities that led to their past success. We've all heard the adage, "Past success is the best predicator of future success." Yet, when we operate from this limited view of "more of what worked before," we leave our greatest potentiality on the table—namely, the vast capacity for creativity, wisdom, intuition, and hidden gifts we can access and develop when we tap into the exponential intelligence available within and beyond us.

To put it simply: best practices have not made room for Soul.

It's time for the "and." For the harmony of internal and external intelligence. For already-developed gifts and latent gifts ready to emerge. For the best of the visible and proven to support the best of the emerging and unproven. The next era of "highest potential" and "best practice" includes our Soul.

During my "in-between" time, I did not know how to bridge that delta. Instead, I filled the gap with other things. Books. Cooking. Wine. Travel of the kind that involved no meetings or deadlines. I took great pleasure in being able to revive my relationship to fun.

One day, I decided—as part of my ongoing experiment—to accept a friend's invitation to join her for a yoga class. I had literally been putting her off for years: no time, no interest, not intense enough for this Type-A gal. Trouble was, I no longer had the excuse of my chronic busyness to fall back on.

It was not at all usual for me to show up to anything so uninformed, unprepared, and unpracticed. I had no clue what the Sanskrit names for the *asanas* (yoga poses) meant; only regular peeks at my neighbors on the mats to my left and right kept me on track. And can you say *inflexible*? Everyone else seemed to move gracefully from one posture to the next. Me? Not so much. My inner critic was on hyper-alert, and spent the whole class pointing out my lack of competence.

In the end, I survived. After class, the teacher approached me. "One day," she said, with total certainty, "you will be teaching this class."

I wanted to laugh at the sheer improbability of me teaching yoga. *Oh my goodness, Punkin,* I thought. *I'm only here because my friend prodded me for three years and bribed me with good wine.* Nevertheless, a seed was planted.

Week after week, I was drawn to return to that class. I still felt awkward and struggled with the physical part of practice, yet my growing enthusiasm surpassed both my lack of skill and my discomfort with not being "good enough." My lifelong pattern of curiosity and information-seeking was on fire—however, for the very first time, I was focusing all that energy on the integration of my mind, body, and spirit, and not on some outside goal.

Never before had I encountered anything like this—not in graduate school, not in Cognitive Behavior Therapy trainings, and certainly not amongst my circle of family, friends, and colleagues (which was full of nurses, physicians, social workers, and executives). I felt like I was learning something beyond the regarded data or approaches I had relied upon, although the knowledge I was gaining was so intuitive, so non-linear, that I couldn't even describe it, let alone communicate it to others.

A couple months later, I decided to jump feet-first (literally) into a nine-month Yoga teacher training certification. Shortly after, I also undertook a Reiki Master certification. The more I learned about energy and the integration of mind, body, and spirit, the more I wanted to know. Whole worlds were unfolding before me—and they were all, simultaneously, *within* me.

I began to remember the way I was as a child. Gardening with Grandma Marion, climbing trees, biking, swimming, running barefoot and free. Outside and alive, in both scorching heat and frigid winters. What had happened to my love of nature? Through the years, I'd organized short stops on my business trips—a few hours among the local landscapes, just long enough to gape in awe and wonder at the beauty of our planet before dashing off to the next meeting.

Nature once again began to take a prominent place in my life, only this time it was my companion and teacher in expanded learning. I walked, hiked, and swam. I lost myself in the land. I showed up with the intention of staying present. I practiced delaying the logical solve. I asked questions of the trees, the earth, the sky.

And I listened. Really listened.

What I didn't expect was how and where the answers to my questions—both spoken and unspoken—began to arise. Honestly, I wasn't sure what the heck was going on. Waves of intuition, deep inner knowing, downloads of information I had not been accessing ... these all became part of my daily routines. Above all, I discovered a sense of being connected to something greater than myself. Even though I did not yet define what this "something greater" was, I was aware I was tapping into a greater consciousness—a universal consciousness both within me and beyond me.

Much later, I learned that science—particularly in the areas of consciousness research and quantum physics—is starting to confirm the idea of universal energy and intelligence. Yet in the moment, none of my prior competencies or capabilities could give me the slightest bit of context for what was going on. My dearly held paradigms were not just being expanded, they were being obliterated. I wasn't just a human. I was a spiritual being in a temporary human suit. A Soul on a mission.

When my year of exploration was over, I knew I was no longer the same person I had been when I said yes to that severance package. I was wearing her skin, but within, I was different.

I knew my Soul was not done with me; I was still in that in-between place, although in a different zip code (or maybe on a different planet) than where I'd started. Still, I told myself, I couldn't play forever. It was time to get back to work.

I played around a bit with consulting, focusing on my past experiences with cultural change and leadership assessments. Rather quickly, I determined it wasn't a good fit. I was "neti-neti"—not quite this, not quite that. Not quite traditional corporate, not yet confident enough to integrate the cosmic, mystical world I was exploring into my business.

So, I got a job.

It was so different this time. I remember clearly the day when—in the midst of a high-stress, multi-country, carve-out divestiture I was co-leading for Human Resources—one of my coworkers turned to me and said, "Why are you always so happy? How do you do it?"

Oh, the irony.

On the one hand, I was indeed happi*er*. My year of play and reconnection to family and friends, fused with my new exploration of energy, ancient wisdom, and cutting-edge science, had brought me to a place of harmony and groundedness I had never experienced before. My work hours no longer consumed my days *and* nights. Yet, the biggest shift was that I was able to keep the nonstop crises at work firmly in perspective. I knew the world wouldn't stop if I didn't respond instantaneously or live in a state of eternal readiness, chained to my devices.

Don't get me wrong, the fire in my belly was still very much alive. However, leading my teams to deliver excellence and giving my entire life to a project were two different things. My bigger purpose in life—even though I still wasn't sure what that was—still won out.

But ... *happy?* I wasn't sure.

Grateful, yes.

Feeling fully alive, on-fire, and in peace? No.

Something was still missing. The yearning and restlessness were still there. My quest for spiritual awareness and growth wasn't complete. More, I was hiding those parts of myself every day. I put on my corporate suit, played nice, followed the written and unwritten rules (well, mostly), and pretended my world hadn't been blown wide open. By night, I often left my body in expansive meditative experiences.

Not surprisingly, the inner whispers once again became deafeningly loud. Over and over, I was awake in the middle of the night with my thoughts running nonstop. In the brief moments when they relented, my Soul whispered: *It's time to leave.*

I'd been thinking that for months—and yet, here I was again, reluctant to take the leap into the unknown. *Seriously... again? How about in a couple of years?*

As it does, the universe stepped in. My job was restructured. I declined the position I was offered, knowing there was too large a gap between what was required and who I had become.

It was time to be more of *me*. Living. Speaking. Being.

Well, it was time to be *closer* to all of that, at least.

I started a coaching and consulting business focused on solution sets that were traditionally "proven" to unleash potential—at least, in the way "potential" was understood within corporate walls. By all outward measures, it was successful, with a steady pipeline of referrals fueled by my Fortune 50 background and reputation. Excellence is always a guiding principle for me, so I did my best to deliver beyond what was expected. Clients were elated with their results. All should have been well.

Yet, it wasn't. There was still an incongruency, fortified by fear. I was afraid to deliver the broader, deeper solutions that I knew with every bone in my body were part of the next evolution of human potential. I worried it was too soon to go big with this assertion. Advancing business through harnessing *all* of who we really are, and all that we are capable of becoming when we tap into the expanded potentiality of Soul … that wasn't even close to being on the radar of those I served, and it certainly wasn't part of any "best practices" I knew. *Surely*, I thought, *if I told my clients what I have experienced and am learning, it would crush my business and reputation. Then what?*

Still, here and there, I started to weave in Soul expansion with clients who were receptive. Holy wow! Those sessions were *fire*. Clients began achieving beyond anything they had experienced before. More, they began to tune into their own deeper wisdom and Soul callings—sources they had not known existed or hadn't yet learned to trust. In those moments, they felt more alive than ever—and so did I.

And then, there was the rest of my business. I still felt unsafe to come out of the spiritual "closet" with most of my clients. When I tentatively introduced these new possibilities to people who had known me in my old roles, I was more often than not met with raised eyebrows and a quizzical, "What the heck *happened* to you, Thomps?"

Over time, those less receptive clients faded away. Referrals started drying up. Big client contracts instantly evaporated in M&A transitions. And the more I tried to take "safe" action, the faster things unraveled. My whole future felt at risk; I feared my business wouldn't survive if this continued. But if it survived as it was—with me continuing to deny what I was learning and who I was becoming—well, that would almost be worse.

Deep down, I knew I was the one stepping on the hose. The identity I was trying to hold on to—the acceptable, polished coach who fit so perfectly into the corporate culture—was getting harder and harder to maintain. My real gifts to leaders, entrepreneurs, and executives were not traditional. They were not the established offerings that could be obtained from thousands of other (well-qualified and talented) people. That wasn't what I had been put here on Earth to do. I had always been on the cutting edge, even in my pre-corporate days as a mental health psychotherapist. Why was I so scared to take a stand now?

I invested massively during this time, seeking out other coaches and experts to help me grow my business. I tried to create and sell the kinds of "mainstream" products other coaches were making tons of money on. Nada. Nothing would take flight. Even all the "right" moves couldn't stop me from falling now.

Living in half-congruence was simply not working. I got by with it for a while—many of us do. But it was exhausting—physically, mentally, and emotionally. Listening to and acting from fear-based thoughts was clearly not working. Eventually, I came to the point where they only thing left to do was let go, and tune in.

I knew that there were solutions, support, and wisdom I wasn't tapping into. I could sense them. So, I began again. Going inward. Listening. Asking. Noticing. Acting on the guidance I received, and trusting my own truths.

And, to no surprise, my business— and, more importantly, my whole life—began to thrive.

I know now that I could have made this shift into congruency earlier, if I hadn't been clinging so tightly to my former identity. The more I anchored in my fears of failure and rejection, the more disconnected I became from my true source of power. Only when I had depleted every outer solution was I drawn inward.

We are not alone in this dance. But how, in those moments of fear and uncertainty, do we let go of the parts of ourselves that are seeking to die?

The Art *of the* Pause

When you answer a 911 from your Soul, it's likely that you will be drawn into what I call "The Pause"—that foggy space between where you were and where you will be next. Your Pause may look different than mine, and one thing is certain: it will make you squirm. Maybe, like me, you will try to move into "fix-it" mode and fill the gaps with anything that shuts off your tyrannical inner critic. Or, maybe, you'll experience temporarily waves of paralysis from fear and indecision and feel unable to move at all. I did, too.

Although it may not feel that way, both are common; sometimes both are even necessary as a catalyst to growth. Unsettling? Definitely. Uncomfortable? Absolutely. Yet, when you are down on your knees, metaphorically or literally, you are drawn *in,* and you open to a greater way.

The Pause is all about being *in* life. Being *all* in, with full sensory experience—as in, really hearing, seeing, smelling, touching, tasting, breathing, and *listening*. It requires you to be in your body, feel all the feels, be with what is, and rest in the not-knowing—versus trying to tidy up, run away, shut down, or escape.

The tropes are true: the only way out is in.

The more you lean into life, the more difficult you will find it to delude yourself about this. Once you've seen what is waiting for you in the Pause—a glimpse, or a revelation, of a greater truth, connection, and purpose—you can't unsee it. You will always feel it, waiting patiently, for you to answer the call.

You may be wondering: how did we forget how to *be* in life in the first place? How in the world did the thing that is supposed to be the easiest, most natural state to occupy become so far from the norm? And, most of all, how has the purported path to happiness—the paradigm of success and achievement that we are all spoon-fed from birth—left us with so many longings that run so deep?

How is success *not enough?*

We   especially those of us who fall into the category of "high achievers"—are taught to succeed at all costs. Although that is not literally spoken (most of the time), this drive toward success is etched into the fabric of our being. Inadvertently, the dream of future freedom is pursued at the expense of living a fully free and *alive* life today.

Whether we pursue this ideal of success through traditional education and ladder-climbing, or through less-traditional pathways (i.e., social media platforms), we still chase it. The houses, the cars, the vacations, the clothes, the prestige … they're the rewards that keep us on script. Yet, playing the game doesn't put us on a path to some glorious destination. It keeps us on a treadmill. The very things that were meant to liberate us become shackles.

Turns out, we've been set up.

And at the same time, it's all to our advantage.

You see, we are all students in Earth School. And having our life plan, identity, or expectations turned upside down by a 911 from our Soul is actually preparing us for our next evolution.

"Earth School" is the physical canvas of human life—a forum where a bunch of events, people, ideas, and paradigms interact and play out according to many scripts. It's like a big playground of lessons. On that playground, you'll get to meet many characters: some, you'll like instantly and be thrilled to have met, while others you may wish never to see again. You'll also have a chance to play out situations that are both joyful and challenging, often with unknown props. Unbeknownst to us is that every fellow student, every game, and every obstacle on the course is part of our growth assignment. Sometimes the lessons and experiences are decadent, and we want them to last forever. Others are challenging and quite painful. Yet at some point in time, some beauty is revealed out of even the darker times.

In Earth School, you'll receive similar recurring lessons until you learn what is required to accelerate to the next level—a new perspective, a new experience of connection and love, or a new way of moving through the world. If you've ever had the same relationship play out with three different partners, or the same challenges arise in different job settings, you'll recognize this pattern. However, what we often forget is that we get to co-direct our own curriculum. We choose what we say yes to, what we reject, and what we save for later. If events unfold that are not by your choice, you still get to choose how you navigate them.

The one thing you *can't* do in Earth School is opt out of learning. The lessons will keep coming until you are ready to engage with them. There's a cost to playing small and denying your true nature. However, once you choose to take the path of remembrance—of holy reassembly—you will be given innumerable signs and support to guide you on your journey.

By design, we are in search of the sacred. Somewhere along the way, we've all forgotten this; in fact, we forgot that we're in Earth School at all. That's okay. Actually, it's part of the curriculum.

When a 911 pulls you into "The Pause"—when you can no longer rise above the blocks, and when "best practices" no longer work—you are being called into the classroom of life to unlock your answers and your path. Your Soul is your teacher, and it will show you how to move through life using the wisdom of your heart and the power of love in service to a greater plan.

Yes, there's something bigger going on here. And you are a necessary, incredible, irreplaceable part of it.

Your 911 is the gateway to this understanding.

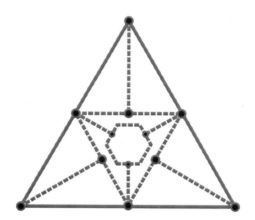

Chapter 3

Meeting Yourself

Once you know a truth, you can't un-know it.

If you allow yourself to be with this new, expanded truth, the intelligence of life will usher you to the next step of revealing and unfolding. One foot in front of the other. Feeling and sensing your way through the unknown.

Right now, you are standing on a precipice of truth. You can choose to ignore your 911 and the ways in which life is speaking to you. Or, you can recognize that something is being moved through you and for you, and open to that which is seeking to reveal itself through your experience.

From where you stand, fear may seem deafeningly loud. It certainly was for me as I navigated my own 911. Yet, as big as the fear felt, my desire to serve in a new way was bigger.

In fact, it was gigantic. I could no longer live in incongruency. I could no longer deny who I was becoming, and who I had always been.

There's a big difference between being genuinely unaware and being in flat-out denial. Many of us have naively walked paths in life that we later realized were not serving us, or others, well. But wishing you didn't know because you feel unequipped or underprepared, taking half-steps when Soul is asking you to leap, shoving the truth into the darkest corner of your inner cupboards and burying it with "shoulds" … well, the cost is quite different.

Your Soul knows when the time has come to grow and change. If you insist that you are too busy, that the timing stinks, that the truth is messy and upsetting, that things will magically get better if you just pretend all is well … those are the times when a 911 comes knocking. You cannot hide from your Soul.

We all know this, deep down. And yet, we are clever, creative, and downright skilled at avoiding that which we don't want to know, see, and address. We distract, numb, deflect, ignore, or seek commiseration; each of us has our preferred avoidance tactic.

Personally, I was outstanding at finding the bright side in everything. In me, perpetual positivity met a refined skill of rationalization. During "round two" of my 911, I identified every solid, rational reason why I should not own my truths, and then made those reasons "right" and sunny and nice feeling. I *couldn't* create a Soul-led model that ran counter to current tried-and-true coaching methods. I was a single mom. I had responsibilities. I couldn't put our stability at risk by offering something corporations and leaders weren't ready for. Besides, there were people who loved my old model; I could just dial that up again.

For a long time, I would wake up every morning at 3:33 a.m. Praying, listening, traveling beyond my body ... all that was great, but how about a clue? A plan? Something obvious to tell me, "Do this, don't do that"?

Safety, Punkin. How about that? Could you please put the "growth" on hold, just this once?

A funny thing happens when you ask for Soul guidance and open up with true receptivity—you receive. It's not always what you expect; usually, it's way better, and sometimes it's the polar opposite of what you thought you needed.

I'd love to share some riveting story about "The Moment Everything Changed and My 911 Ended" ... yet this piece of my story is actually rather ordinary. *Lean in. Learn a little bit. Head out on the Earth School playground. Crack the code on that lesson—or don't. Rinse and repeat.*

It was hard, and humbling. Soul often asked me to hang on when it seemed my whole life and identity was dangling by a thread. My habit of looking like I had it all together was fraying like an old coat. And while in the grand scheme of my life—let alone in the grand scheme of humanity—it may have seemed like my struggles at that time were small, even insignificant, they brought me to my knees. I wasn't just being asked to act differently. Soul was asking me to *be different.*

A major thread running through all 911s is a shift of identity. In my in-between, I knew the understandings and beliefs that had carried me through my life and contributed to my joys, successes, love (both lost and found), and pains. These were deeper than my acquired best practices and strategies; they were *who I knew myself to be*, and they had worked more or less sufficiently to this point. And yet ... who was I now?

I hadn't understood before how much of my identity was wrapped up in my role as an executive—the big job, the salary beyond anything my younger self could have imagined, the titles and promotions, the cars and clothes and vacations. All of these reinforced the notion that I was on the "right" path. Layer on others' points of view around what was "respectable" and what constituted "good work," and my own sense of growing older and wanting to make the most of this crazy, precious life ... well, who I was being was no longer who I *needed* to be to live as my Soul was calling me to live.

I dove into exploration like my life depended on it. I took courses in everything from energy work to diverse traditions, wisdom texts and philosophies to modern-day mysticism. I worked with shamans, healers, spiritual mentors, and equine guided self-discovery. I visited sacred sites. I explored many paths and many perspectives ... and in the end, they all led me back to myself, and the call I was being offered by Soul.

Eventually, through many stops and starts, I was given a glimpse of what Soul wanted to move through me and for me. And it was more profound and beautiful than I could have imagined.

In Search *of the* Sacred

A 911 is a Soul crisis, and a Soul crisis is a spiritual crisis.

At the core of a 911 is a search for the sacred—what is sacred for you, in you, around you, and beyond you. You are looking for the parts of yourself you *feel* are there, yet somehow you lost connection with. A search for the sacred is a search for the truth of who you are and who you are meant to become.

You are embarking on a quest to meet yourself.

For me this was not a religious quest. Similarly, many of the people I meet who have been propelled on this journey via their own 911s are those whom researchers call "The Nones"—people who claim no religious identity. Searching for the sacred within and around you may or may not include searching for (the popular definitions of) God, the universe, angels, spirit guides, or other benevolent helpers—however, a common underpinning of a Soul quest is a search for connection to, and reunification with, the divine consciousness within, around and beyond you.

How you define that divine consciousness is highly personal; your religious beliefs may inform that exploration. Soul and Spirit are the best words I currently have to offer you context and understanding of your 911 and the identity shift that is wanting to occur as a result; therefore, those are the words I've used throughout this book. You may decide to refer to your inner divine consciousness as God, Goddess, The universe, Source, your Higher Self, or something else entirely—and if any or all of those words carry unhelpful baggage for you, don't use them. Instead, find language that works for you and feels resonant. If you're not sure, test and try.

The "holy reassembly" which occurs when we reconnect with Soul and reclaim the parts of ourselves that we have denied (or been unaware of) will, by design, reveal our deepest personal truths. Each of us has a path to walk, and our paths will be unique and different than the paths of others. However, all of us who pursue this invitation, whether through deliberate seeking or the invitation of a 911, will at some point be brought face to face with ourselves. In this meeting, we will discover more about our connection to life—how life is moving in service to us, and how we can be in service to life. This interconnectedness, alignment, and feeling of purpose—for your life, and for all life—is at the heart of what many of us are seeking without knowing it.

Yet, how can we trust this holy reassembly and tune in to the voice of Soul when we are successful, driven, "Type A," multi-tasking, fix-it-and-move-on machines? More, how can we allow our definitions of success to change? How can we accommodate and integrate what our Soul is preparing to move through us? How can we value our accomplishments and goals while honoring what is truly sacred for us?

These are just some of the many questions that arise along the progressive journey. The answers are yours to uncover and enliven.

We all come from different traditions, beliefs, and ways, with roots in vast locations and perspectives. And still, as individuals residing in different communities and countries, we are all on a similar path toward understanding who we are, and who we are called to be, individually and collectively.

We don't need more strategies, formulas, and dogmatic how-tos. We need a way to guide and inform the process of living our highest expression in and through all seasons of life.

The Soul Solution

Once you recognize what your 911 is actually inviting you into, and recognize that you are seeking your own sacred nature, it's time to enter the space of unknowing—the space between who you were and who you are becoming.

Holy wow. We are not taught how to meet the unknown with ease. I was taught to use my head and "just flipping figure it out." Most of us were—yet that won't help us answer the call.

Even after years of seeking and searching, making space to hear Soul's voice was new to me. Not surprisingly, I responded with resistance, avoidance, and digging my heels in. I looked for *acceptable* practices that would support me in this identity shift that would keep me aligned with my executive coaching work even though my heart was no longer in it. The harder things got, the more determined I was to figure it out in my head—and sometimes in other people's (by asking experts what they thought). It was predominately all head.

Heart? Well, that was rarely part of the dialogue back then. There may have been core values hanging on the walls for all to see, yet my clients reported what was modeled lacked congruency.

Do what it takes to deliver the expected results? Of course.

Consider your broader life, feel like you matter, and be

truly seen, heard, and valued? Not so much.

Rely on the intelligence of Heart, Soul, and "knowings" from beyond? *Are you kidding, Thomps? We've got a business to run.*

During my time in corporate leadership, I was blessed to have a CEO and leadership team who were way ahead of their time when it came to honoring the unique contributions of all employees. Answers could be found anywhere; not everything was a top-down, title-led approach. Diversity of ideas and expression was invited and celebrated. Did we get it right all the time? No, we did not. Still, there was a ton of heart in the company. I have treasured relationships to this day with many former coworkers, shaped by the deep connections and support, and by the feeling that we were all part of something that mattered.

There can be a place for Soul in both life and business—and there are many who are open to that invitation. Even so, the opportunity your 911 is bringing forth, and the opportunity I am bringing forth in this book, is beyond what has been previously available. It's the inclusion of the deeper Spiritual Heart, where expanded intelligence and untapped gifts can be received in service to individuals, companies, communities, and the planet.

These days I see so many spiritually-infused quotes like "Listen to your heart," or "You've sold your soul to your job" posted on forums like LinkedIn. They are highly viewed; many people "like" or "love" them. There is a craving there that hasn't yet been named, a desire to bring real connection, appreciation for the whole of who you are, hope, and inspiration into a space that has historically been dedicated to logic, metrics, and results. Still, when it comes to actually listening to our Heart or reclaiming our Soul from exile? That still feels far out of line with what's expected or outlined in most business protocols.

Eventually, through a lot of trial and error, I came to see that my resistance to my True Self—and not living aligned with my Soul, Mind, Body, Heart, Gratitude, Service, and Love—prompted me to make decisions that attracted the very things I was trying to avoid. I was looking for the wrong things in the wrong places, doing work that was no longer aligned with my gifts and passions, and causing myself increasing financial and spiritual distress. *Note to self: the energy in which you make a decision will be highly correlated to the outcome you are creating.*

Moving from, and as, Love became far more meaningful and powerful for me than the cultural ideology so well grooved into my brain and way of being. I recognized that I was in search of something more than a new way of working, or even a new way of being. I was in search of the sacred within me and around me. I wanted to be connected to something bigger—to a bigger purpose, a bigger plan, a higher intelligence, and the fullness of *all* I came here to be. And each of the signs I had received in the form of struggle, adversity, confusion, and resistance were pointing me in the direction of my Soul all along.

I have come to understand and characterize two broad ways of seeing life, myself, and the world. There is the "Earth View," the conditioned and very human way in which we process life on a daily basis, and "Soul View," the expanded, integrated viewpoint of higher intelligence. Each has a place in the grander scheme of my life—yet in order for me to access the full range of gifts available to me, I need to harmonize them in such a way that I can live more from, and as, Soul while traversing Earth School in a human suit.

I now call this place of integration "the beauty of the 'and.'" On the other side of this learning curve, the processes I had moved through became crystallized. Along this wild, not-at-all linear journey, I nevertheless accessed seven clear spiritual principles, each a facet of my human and spiritual existence. In each, I had been asked to find the beauty of the "and," and allow space for both Earth View and Soul View to share their wisdom.

These seven principles, which I collectively call The Soul Solution, are the core of this book, and the heart of all the work I do with my clients today. They provide a blueprint for daily living as you invite the truth of who you are to come forward and take the helm in your life. They are statements to live by, and also deep wells of wisdom we can unpack to create greater coherence between your truest nature and your human experience.

THE SOUL SOLUTION

I align with my Soul to discover my truth

I direct my Mind in service of my Soul

I honor my Body as the vehicle of my Soul

I tune into my Heart to illuminate the way

I generate Gratitude for all that was, is, and will be

I live in Service to life, and life is in service to me

I am Love, and say yes to leading with love

In Part II of this book, we will examine the Earth View and Soul View of each of the seven principles and uncover the wisdom and gifts of each.

Again, these are not theoretical or religious axioms; rather, they are invitations into your own truths. And while I will offer suggestions to help you explore and live each of these principles as you move through your 911, I ultimately encourage you to make them come alive in ways that align with what is resonant for you.

For me, the seven principles of The Soul Solution enable me to live my truth with more clarity, confidence, integrity, and ease, while also tapping into potentiality beyond what I knew was available to me. I am finally realizing and taking responsibility for the dreams sewn into my Heart and the role I am meant to play as an embodied Soul.

This is ever evolving, and it's meant to be—not just for me, but for all of us. My own 911 gave me the compassion, vision, and experience needed to be a teacher to others on this path—to be a "matchmaker" reuniting humans with their Souls and highest selves.

And so, here we are.

As I shared in the Introduction, I would never in a million years have imagined that *this* is where the wave of my 911 would carry me—and yet, I couldn't imagine living, teaching, and working any other way. I was summoned to dial up the courage and vulnerability necessary to say, "This is who I am, what I believe, and how I serve. Here I AM."

THE STORY OF YOUR 911

Now that I've walked you through my own journey and to the other side of my 911, you may have some inkling of what Soul is calling you toward in your own life.

The stories we tell ourselves about our 911 are, ultimately, just as meaningful as the 911 itself. The meanings we choose to make from events, feelings, and relationships actually determine how we see ourselves and our lives, and how we move through the Earth School playground.

Before you move on from this chapter, I encourage you to get a pen and journal (or the voice note app on your phone) and capture what you tell yourself about your own 911.

You've told the story to yourself, sometimes many times. You may have told it (or portions of it) to others, too. Write or speak whatever arises without filters or judgment.

If you're not currently experiencing a 911, you can choose any area of your life where there is a gap between what is and what you desire.

Be sure to touch on the following points and feel free to add whatever you'd like:

- Describe the 911(i.e., what happened?)
- What is the current situation?
- What are your "what ifs"? (What if X happens? Or, If X, then Y …)
- What common thoughts do you have about this 911?

- What feelings are you experiencing? Which are strongest?

- What steps have you already taken?

- What actions have you not taken? What makes it challenging to act?

- How do you talk to yourself about this 911? (i.e., with compassion, blame)

- What do you think this means for your future (near- and long-term)?

- How would you like this to turn out?

After you capture your story, set your journal or device aside. Breathe in deeply, feel your belly expand, and exhale fully as you feel the return of your belly. Invite this life force gift of breath to move through your whole system. 3-5 rounds will be goodness.

We will be returning to this practice in future chapters so please save these initial reflections.

Step *into* Soul

Today, we are more connected than ever across the globe and to our family and friends—and, at the same time, we are more disconnected than ever. There are so many things vying for our attention. We turn to our devices, online experts, and social media for connection and direction, and increasingly we are becoming more lost, confused, lonely, and distracted from our true nature and the nature of one another.

Whether we know it or not, we deeply crave a return to what has been available all along—the truth, hidden in plain sight, that is summoning us home.

I'm so glad you are here, my friend.

Come with me.

There is a Soul you are longing to meet.

Part II

The Soul Solution

Welcome, Dear One.

Come, rest in the arms of love.

You are safe.

You are whole.

You are so much more than you know yourself to be.

It is time to remember who you are.

Welcome home.

Chapter 4

I align with my Soul to discover my truth.

"If only they knew ..."

Five minutes into our bimonthly coaching call, Natalia could no longer hold back the waterfall of tears. "It's all falling apart," she sobbed. "And no one has any idea."

My heart ached for her. She was one of the strongest, most accomplished women I'd ever met—and maintaining her success was tearing her apart.

Natalia and I had connected for executive integration. She was looking for support as she transitioned to a new C-suite role with a major tech company. Her CEO and peers believed she was abundantly qualified (and she was), and she thrived in her role (to no one's surprise but her own). However, despite this glowing new chapter in her story of success, she felt like she was in over her head. More, she felt vulnerable, overwhelmed, and at risk—as if, at any moment, someone might find out that she really didn't deserve to be in this top-of-the-house role and expose her as a fraud. Natalia, like many leaders, struggled with imposter syndrome. She felt like everyone else had it all figured out at work and at home, and doubted her own talents, accomplishments, and ability. She often wondered: how did she rise to this level at all?

From the outside, Natalia's life was impressive, even enviable. She was at the pinnacle of her expertise, a sought-after leader in her field. She was smart, funny, fit, and always meticulously put together. She had married her college sweetheart, a well-known entrepreneur, and their thirty-year partnership was the envy of everyone in their circle. Their three adult children were all thriving in their post-college careers. She lived in her dream home near the ocean. She drove beautiful cars. She traveled internationally.

And most of all, she was kind. Empathetic. Always "on" for others, whether at work or at home. She was loved.

Yet, as is so often the case, the shiny picture observed from the outside did not reflect what was really going on. In Natalia's case, there was a significant disconnect—and it was literally tearing her apart.

Admired by others for "having it all," Natalia felt immense pressure and was struggling to keep up the façade. She was skilled at rising to the occasion, taking care of whatever arose in the moment—however, she was doing so at the expense of herself. In the rare moments when she wasn't dashing from one demanding situation to another, she still couldn't relax. Her inner critic was screaming at her, highlighting her deficiencies, and reminding her that it would only take one careless gesture to knock down the whole house of cards.

Her "ideal" marriage was on the verge of implosion—physically intact, but emotionally and intimately bankrupt. She suspected her husband was having an affair, since his absences from home were becoming steadily longer than what his work travel usually demanded. When she confronted him, he turned on the charisma and convinced her she was just imagining things. She desperately wanted to believe him—to believe that the dream was still real—but her inner knowing wouldn't let her pretend any longer.

On top of that, her friends frequently called her in a panic with recurring relational and financial crises that only Natalia could resolve. This pattern of being the "rescuer" was not new; even as a child, she had felt responsible for everyone and everything around her, from keeping her mom happy, to getting good grades so her dad would be proud, to maintaining perfect dress and manners so as not to "bring shame" to the family.

Boundaries? They were non-existent. And asking for help? Not a chance. She had it all. Who was she to ask for support? Being on the receiving side was foreign to her. How could she even begin to ask for what she needed? It felt like the asking would confirm her fears that she wasn't enough.

Yet Soul, as it often does, was about to make the asking inevitable. Natalia had been diagnosed just days before with adrenal fatigue and Hashimoto's Disease. After years of refusing to advocate for herself, her body was speaking for her. If she didn't listen to this 911, her intense symptoms could become even more debilitating.

As we looked into each other's eyes that day, she let me see it all: the fear, the insecurity, the feeling that it was all too much, and that life would never stop demanding the impossible from her.

"I have nothing more to give," she said. "My body is done. My heart is done. Where do I go from here?"

"Natalia," I said, gently. "Your Soul is speaking. *Loudly*. You've put a lid on what you've desired for so long. You've kept all the balls in the air for everyone else. What if it's time to ask what *you* want? It's time to reconnect with and reclaim your true nature. Who you really are already knows your truths and the best path forward."

I went on to share that, on both a conscious and unconscious level, Natalia was betraying herself. She had been for years. She denied the truths that flashed on her inner radar— both in her marriage, and in her professional world. She denied herself the love and nurturing she needed to feel safe, whole, and supported; instead, she operated from the outmoded belief that it was her responsibility to take care of others under all circumstances. Desperately trying to keep all of the various balls in the air and uphold her public persona, she had forgotten what it meant to plant her feet on the solid ground of her truth. Over time, slowly but surely, her false foundation had eroded. She'd lost her relationship with herself, and the person she knew herself to be.

Self-betrayal is common in general, and highly successful people are no exception. As we try to escape our fears of failure, humiliation, and mediocrity, we move further and further from who we are. It happens, not all at once, rather in a series of small moments. It's sneaky, almost invisible—until we find ourselves in a 911.

What Natalia longed for was *freedom*. Freedom from the ever-increasing demands from her job and friends. Freedom from her sham of a marriage. Freedom from the internal story that she should have done more, tried harder, been better. In search of that freedom, she had attended countless webinars, seminars, and retreats. She'd read books on leadership, courage, self-love, and spirituality. Yet this feeling of fragility was more than her mind could handle. She needed more than just a theoretical understanding that there was something more to life.

She had heard her 911 loud and clear. Now, the healing could begin.

The work Natalia and I did together began with the process we are about to undertake in this chapter: to find Soul under the multiple layers of not-Soul (false self) that have accumulated, like sediment, over the course of your life. It's not a discovery process; it's an excavation. The revealing and remembering of what has been within you all along.

What *is* Soul?

Like so many high achievers, "living my highest potential" has been a lifelong passion for me.

For decades, I researched "maximizing potential." I strove to be in the "top box" in corporate environments. I took classes, worked with mentors, hired coaches ... you know the drill. Whatever the buzz words or hot skills of the year were, I learned them, practiced them, took action (and more action) to implement them, and did my best to master them. Even before my executive days, I was always looking for *more*—for myself, and for the clients in my therapy practice.

There's a lot to be said for equipping individuals to live their highest potential. We are coded to evolve. But there's one key point of which many of us—myself included—have lost sight.

The most powerful pathway to potential that exists *is already alive and awake within you now.*

It is, of course, *Soul.*

My understanding of Soul is that it is an eternal essence, a subtle energy frequency which is connected to an invisible grid of universal intelligence. It is, simultaneously, your life (and lives), and the life of the universe. It is a whole and holy expression of *All That Is* (aka, God, Source, Creative Intelligence, The Divine, The universe, The Great Mystery or anything else you choose to call it.)

I don't associate Soul with religion of any kind. As I've heard many teachers say, "You aren't born with religion." We are given religion through instruction; it is shaped not by Soul, but by our human community. Yet, of the over 4,000 religions, each have beliefs about what Soul is or is not. We are wired to search for the sacred—and religions give us some possible pathways to do that. However, they aren't the *only* pathways.

While religious beliefs may or may not inform your personal approach, what is most important is *the experience* with and of Soul, not the word ascribed to it.

In Greek philosophy there is a concept explored by Aristotle and others called "entelechy"—the vital principle that governs the development of an organism. It is the *entelechy* of an acorn to become an oak tree. It is the *entelechy* of a caterpillar to become a butterfly. Nature innately knows who to become and what to do. You, too, are coded with a seed of potential—everything you need to realize your highest and best expression. It doesn't happen automatically, yet it is there, and under the right conditions, it can be nurtured and expanded. It is the *entelechy of Soul to realize* your highest potential, already resident within you, available and waiting for you to nurture its fullest expression.

In preparation to write this book, I asked my clients, friends, and business contacts from around the world what "Soul" meant to them. Here are a few of the answers I received:

- The Soul is eternal and lives on beyond the death of my body.
- The Soul lives within the physical body.
- The Soul is an essence experienced, but not in the body.
- Soul is an inner knowing that I am so much larger and part of the larger cosmic experience.
- Soul is where I paint from.
- Soul is what I feel when I listen to certain music.

- Soul is my Higher Self.

- The Soul within is a god-seed likeness and connected to a higher power or transcendent God, Spirit, or universal energy.

- Soul is what I feel when I close my eyes and know that I AM.

- I don't relate to that word at all, but I relate to the experience of Soul like during times of creative flow free of ego, access to deeper potential and wisdom.

- Soul is my being, and part of the collective whole.

- Soul is that niggling feeling of intuition when I *know* something but don't know how or why I know it.

In the Practice section of this chapter, you will find an exercise to capture your personal understanding of Soul. Even if "Soul" is not a word you relate to or use, I invite you to open to your own experience of the concept and create a meaning around it that feels resonant to you.

WHAT YOUR SOUL KNOWS

Your Soul knows you are not your body. It knows you *have* a body, and it desires for your body, mind, and personality to come into alignment with it. Soul is the guiding force toward the highest and purest expression of All That Is that is seeking to be realized through you. Your Soul knows why you are here in this physical embodiment, what choices are best for you, and the most direct routes to take to live a wildly delicious and fulfilling life. It knows where the treasures are hidden along the way, and what learnings and evolutions await you en route along your progressive journey. It knows where you will go, why you will go there, and who you are capable of being as an individual and as a microcosm of the collective.

As a Soul, you have access to an infinite warehouse of wisdom on any topic. This innate knowledge empowers you to solve any problem, anywhere, in any circumstance. It allows you to discern your personal *truth*, as it exists in this moment, over and above the facts or evidence of your material circumstance. Facts iterate and dissolve; they are coded, like us, to evolve. But truth, as it exists to your Soul, isn't about facts; rather, it is about divine knowing. When you align with your truth, it is liberating. More, it is a life-long pursuit, for as you grow and evolve, your truths may as well.

Your Soul is the whisper that says, "All is well," even when the world seems to be falling apart. It's the voice of protest when you squelch your inner knowing in order to fit in or please someone else. It's the courage that the mind cannot muster or sustain. It's the clarity that goes beyond what the five senses can perceive. It's the remembrance that you are more than your five senses, or the body that you wear. It's the genesis of possibilities that far supersede your current situation and what others deem realistic or even possible.

Most of all, your Soul has your back. It wants you to remember that you are loved, and whole. When you connect to your Soul, you will feel embraced. You'll know that you are safe, and that you are enough.

THE EARTH VIEW OF SOUL

You came to this planet for a reason: to learn how to love your-self, to learn how to love others, and to contribute to a better future for humanity. Everything that you have been through, everything that you have experienced (both joys and suffer-ings) is a clue and a catalyst to this greater goal. There are traits and skills within you that are seeking to be developed and expressed, and experiences to be realized.

And, in moments of suffering, it can be awfully hard to remember this.

In the immediacy of navigating a 911, we can forget that everything is happening *for* us, not to us. Even your current 911 has a purpose beyond what you can easily see right now—and how you navigate it will be shaped by your current belief systems and past experiences—what I call the "Earth View."

When your 911 unfolds, you are likely to view your current circumstances through the lens of what has happened, what the evidence tells you is likely to happen next, and what the external world and other people are offering as possible rea-sons or solutions. You might think, "I have to fix these prob-lems, or everything will fall apart!" You might fear the loss of power you predict is looming as a result of this 911—the material, financial, relational, or self-image implications of what is transpiring. Your ego rises up to protect you and the Earth View of this call becomes the "reality."

Control is key in the Earth View of Soul. We drive ourselves batty clinging to the notion that we can control it all—even our

Soul, even God—if only we can be smart and prepared enough. When things get squirrelly, we beat ourselves down with criticism and focus on the unachievable ideal of perfection, *hoping* this will protect us from the change we fear is coming.

As Natalia discovered, we can only build that wall so high before the artificial foundation gives out.

That's why the first step in processing this 911 from your Soul is to remember that you are a Soul having a human experience. Your Soul is not separate from you. You don't have to search for it; it has never left you. While the ego's fuel is fear, the Soul's fuel is love. All that is unfolding widens the channel of communication between your human self and your Soul in service to who you came here to be.

The difference between Soul and ego is that Soul doesn't seek control. Instead, it seeks growth and expression. All is not in our control—and we can absolutely influence what we create, and how we respond.

THE SOUL VIEW OF SOUL

The following wisdom from Thomas Merton, a Trappist monk and scholar of comparative religion, sparked a resounding cord in the wake of my personal 911.

There is in us an instinct for newness, for renewal, for a liberation of creative power. We seek to awaken in ourselves a force which really changes our lives from within. And yet the same instinct tells us that this change is a recovery of that which is deepest, most original, most personal in ourselves. To be born again is not to become somebody else, but to become ourselves.

If you don't have plans to become a monk—or a theologian, for that matter—don't worry. Neither do I. Neither did Edgar Mitchell, an astronaut on the Apollo 14 Moon Mission. Yet, even so, while in space he had a profound experience of oneness and unity with humanity. The view from the moon irrevocably changed how he understood his life, and all of life.

Soul's view of Soul is oneness. Its essence is Spirit. Its vibration is unconditional love, freedom, wisdom, harmony, grace, and light. There is no superiority or inferiority; all are equal.

The body and mind often operate in separation, whereas Soul knows itself in unity. It operates from love and a knowing that the universe is impersonal and governed by not only the laws of science (such as gravity), but also by universal laws (mystical and spiritual) such as oneness, divine paradox, synchronicity, balance, attraction, detachment, karma, and intention and desire.

When we are in opposition to any of these laws, knowingly or unknowingly, life becomes more challenging. The funny thing is, we often reference these laws in daily life. We say things like, "Let it go," or "What goes around comes around," or, "We're all in this together." Because universal laws are not ascribed the same finality as physical laws, they are more easily dismissed—however, as most of us have experienced, the impact of living one's life in contrast is just as painful as attempting to live in opposition to gravity. How many times have you held on desperately to something you knew needed to change, because you wanted what you thought that reality represented ... only to discover that, once you let it go, something even better was waiting in the wings?

The Soul is free of personality and ego. It doesn't fight what is. If you stripped away your personality and ego—if only Soul was looking out through your eyes—you would see a consciousness neither informed nor distracted by human happenings.

In her Reflection Series, *The Courageous Journey of Inner Space*, Caroline Myss references the "jewels" of Soul. She defines these as, "The qualities inherent within the soul that we must awaken within ourselves, such as wisdom, love, trust, faith, endurance, mercy, and judgment/discernment." Can you imagine how life would change if we lived from these jewels with more consistency? If we knew that, while this Earth School gig can be messy and full of uncertainty, we can still choose to operate from trust, truth, and faith?

You have seen examples of humans operating this way. These incredible people demonstrate what seem like impossible acts of love and forgiveness—like the mother who forgave the man who murdered her son (and eventually loved him like another son), or the person who suddenly gained superhuman strength amid a life-and-death situation. Maybe you've even experienced this yourself, in moments that seem to fall completely outside of any human constructs, when grace pours through your human vessel like a river of light.

This is Soul enlivened through us.

THE BEAUTY OF THE "AND"

We are local—here on Earth, in our body—*and* non-local—as a Soul, creative Source energy that is the universe embodied and has access to powers and information beyond the physical. When you pause in the physical world and tune in as awareness, you can perceive both the local and non-local aspects of you and receive the subtle Soul energy that holds greater insights, deeper wisdom, and expanded potential. The art, then, is taking the guidance and translating it into tangible actions in your daily three-dimensional world.

This is what it means to be both finite and infinite.

When you are mired in Earth View, you may feel disempowered, fearful, stuck, or deserving of shame and guilt. You may be immobilized by what is happening around you, or inside you. You may feel like every step feels like a fight, flight or freeze moment.

In contrast, when you are in Soul View, you are able to tune into higher wisdom, receive intuitive promptings, and see the bigger picture. You will feel "nudges" to embody more of your infinite knowledge, skills, and capacity to love. You will feel empowered to ignite momentum and take steps to enliven the Soul view of your situation, even when the logic of Earth School says, "*No flipping way* is that possible."

In each moment, the key is your *willingness* to step forward in trust. Aligning with Soul is a *felt experience* in your body; when you allow it, you become willing to act on Soul's direction even though it may not make logical sense. Time and again, my clients and I have been blown away by what unfolded when they had the courage and faith to act on a knowing or nudge, and how events proved even better than imagined, or created something valuable that hadn't even been on the radar before.

The beauty of the "and" lies in navigating your physical existence from a knowing that you are more than physical. No one is asking you to run away from life to pray in a cave. No one is asking you to give up being who you have become. Your Soul is only asking you to come into the "and"—to rest in the breath and stillness of your infinite self, connect with the greater consciousness of All That Is, and turn down the imperfect information of physicality. You can then walk, talk, work, eat, breathe, sing, dance, and create in physical form knowing that you are acting from a place of your highest and best expression.

You have already connected with the nature of your Soul on Earth—even if you never named it as such until now. Because Earth Views are the predominant views espoused in the media, in books, and even with friends and family, it's sometimes hard to acknowledge or give credence to our experiences with Soul—and that doesn't mean you haven't had them. Maybe you've even experienced a sense that, although your life is being tossed upside down by this current 911, some deeper purpose is being served for you, and through you. Although your current situation may be less than desirable, even painful, when you rest in your Soul awareness, it seems bearable, or even hopeful. You can and will emerge stronger, wiser, and more compassionate from this.

You may have met people who rest in the beauty of the "and." They are likely unbelievably resilient. They're calm and hopeful, even when navigating turbulence and tragedy. While they might feel sad, depressed, or defeated (and allow themselves to experience and express that pain), they don't live in those states. They honor their grief, and even if they don't know what will come after the crisis has passed, they have faith that they will thrive again, albeit differently. The tough experiences are not buried, nor forgotten, but used to inform and shape their perspective in a way that benefits their own and others' lives. Some might call them "Polyannas" or "insanely optimistic," however this isn't spiritual bypassing. When someone truly lives in the beauty of the "and," they are drawing from both the human and the divine parts of themselves; therefore, their experiences also get to be both human and divine.

You are limitless. You are Source energy dressed up in a human body. You are not limited to Earth rules, norms, or conventions. You can co-create and co-direct your experience here. This is true; it is in accordance with universal laws.

In light of this, many wonder if it is possible to live in the space of our unlimited potential every day, in every hour. I'll be honest: I haven't cracked that code. Yet, imagine how life could change if we could fully tap into Soul even 10 percent of the time! There is so much potentiality left on the table every day because we are not leveraging and living all of ourselves.

Natalia found this "and" space when she began to align with Soul to discern her truth and worth, while reimagining what a greater possibility for what her life could be. This empowered her to redefine boundaries and put a stop to her self-betrayal. I found mine when I slowed down enough to hear that quiet inner voice. We all have coping strategies—and one thing is certain, you can't override your 911 from the demands of your ego.

We both yearn for and are intimidated by the power within us—especially during periods where things aren't clear. The beauty of the "and" is that, even when material circumstances are unfolding, we can take comfort in the constant, eternal nature of Soul and trust that we can activate coded intelligence and guidance simply by listening to the messages from within. Life is speaking around us and beyond us, and Soul is always leading us toward our fullest potentiality.

The Voice *of* Your Soul

The voice of your Soul is unique. It has layers and textures that are invisible, yet often more "real" than what we perceive with our senses.

The Soul speaks through your body through sensation and survival-oriented "gut instinct" that alerts you to dangers. The moment your middle tenses up or you feel that crawling sensation in your belly, you know something is off. Even if you're not in imminent danger, this is a clear signal to tune in, reevaluate, and change direction. Conversely, when you erupt in goosebumps, you know you're onto something big!

Soul speaks through *resonance*; when you are being guided, you will know it, or feel it, or both. You will receive percep- tive awareness of decisions or routes that will better serve you.

From "divine downloads" that just seem to drop right through you, to expanded capabilities that, to most, seem impossible for a mere human, Soul's will is animated in your imagination and your physical world. Even when logic and reason don't back up your "knowings," they always work out for you when you follow them.

Often, people will recognize these "Soul hits" as they arise, and simply dismiss them since they don't feel tangible or provable. Only later will they look back and say, "I knew this all along!" Our work, therefore, isn't to "find" our connection to Soul, but rather to trust it in the moment.

Soul also speaks through flow. There are times when life will seem to effortlessly flow to you. Things just seem to line up with ease and joy, and the experiences you desire are realized without forcing or struggle. You might receive clear answers when immersed in a flow state while exercising, painting, playing music, or meditating. When flow is stifled—as mine was when I was living in half-congruence around my business—the opposite occurs. Everything feels like an uphill battle.

Finally, Soul speaks through Nature and the physical world. Symbols, patterns, numbers, vibrations, sound, synchronicities, planetary cycles, and natural phenomena all hold messages and invitations. Soul will implant information in those that feel most important and significant to you.

In future chapters, we'll explore how you can expand your experience of Soul communication. However, as you've likely gathered, Soul's unique potential can only be birthed through the exploration of your interior world. It is revealed in the moments when you let go of your thinking mind and enter Alpha, Theta, or Gamma brain wave states (i.e., meditation or "being in the zone"). At these times, an internal door opens and greater intelligence can move through you. The ways in which this happens will be unique to you—and therefore only truly recognizable by you. Trust them—and trust Soul.

At some time, in some way, all of us will be invited to rediscover who we are and reconnect with Soul. We will be invited to see the greater map of our lives, and understand that everything is, and always has been, part of an interconnected whole. When this happens, we are ready to expand into a new level of love for ourselves, other humans, and all of life.

Nature and the Soul

For a long time, I didn't really connect with nature. When I happened to spend time outside, I was walking at top speed to get fit, not actually being present to what was around me.

After my 911, I learned to root into nature—literally into the Earth herself, walking barefoot on the ground. I learned to connect with the rhythm of the waves' reflections as they lapped the sand or pounded wildly against the rocks. I learned to listen deeply, and ask, "What am I hearing and seeing right now?"

What does this have to do with Soul? Your Soul's brilliance is asking you to *notice*. Out of all the possible landing places in the universe, your Soul chose to come here to Planet Earth, because she is a teacher and a guide for you as well.

When you begin to connect with nature as a teacher and

guide for your Soul, you will begin to see even mundane things from a whole new perspective. The expansiveness of the sky. The fractals in a flower. The shift of the seasons as a dance of renewal and rebirth—and how your body responds to them.

Nature is a soothing balm and nectar. It offers your mind a temporary respite and ignites the jewels of Soul through its beauty and majesty. Give yourself the chance to feel the awe and wonder of a glorious sunset, or the magnetic fury of a thunderstorm. When you are in the midst of a 911, spending time in nature can help you hear Soul's voice more clearly and come out of Earth View with regard to your current situation. In its reflections of the wonderous, Nature helps you remember your true nature.

All around you are examples of interdependency, oneness, and joy. Settle in, and allow yourself to be enveloped in the arms of love—for you, too, are an exquisite expression of the greater whole.

Practices

Right now, you might be thinking, "How on Earth am I going to find the time and energy to do a deep dive into Soul? Even if all the answers *are* actually inside me, I don't have the time and energy to figure this out right now!"

I know that feeling well. And, I remind you: this is *who you already are*. We just need to create the conditions for you to experience more of You (your true nature).

There are countless ways to practice being present and

tuning into Soul. As a start, I'll share a few simple practices. These won't take up a lot of extra time in your day, and I predict that with repetition you'll find you *want* to create more time. The key is to do these practices as often as possible; consistency is more important than length of practice as you begin.

Practice 1: Create Stillness

Stillness is one of the most important and powerful practices you can engage in. This practice is about intentionally creating space to tune into Soul by being with your breath.

If your mind and body are wound up, entering stillness can feel impossible. If this is new to you, no worries. The steps are simple, though they may not feel easy at first. If it is challenging to be still, start with 30-120 seconds of stillness one or two times a day. If creating stillness is familiar, engage for longer   up to twenty minutes or longer each day.

- Find a comfortable place (a chair, a quiet spot in nature, in your car, or even at your desk).
- Set the intention to simply create stillness. You can simply say, "I am still." If you relate to a higher power, you can call on the help of your higher power with the intention.
- Close your eyes and breathe to your own rhythm. Feel the breath in your diaphragm and body.

If subtle messages arise as you sit in stillness, wonderful. However, that is not the goal at this point. If you feel antsy and chaotic thoughts arise, that is normal. Simply redirect your awareness to your belly and notice its expansion and return as you continue to breathe. If your mind is noisy the whole time, that's okay, too. Congratulate yourself on committing to stillness, even if it wasn't still or silent. With time, this practice will get easier.

Practice 2: Be Present

You can practice the art of being present through intentional engagement in simple, repetitive activities that require light focus and don't activate curious thought. Sweeping, mopping, vacuuming, washing dishes slowly, weeding the garden, mowing the lawn, or watering plants are a few examples.

Again, the goal here isn't to seek messages from Soul; rather, it's to hone the practice of being present, which sets the stage for Soul to be heard. The distinction is important. There is no goal but presence and awareness.

Here's how to do it:

- Choose an activity and begin to bring your attention to the experience of whatever you are doing.
- Notice how this activity feels in the body (versus actively thinking about something else as the next to-do list). Notice the rhythm of the broom or mop. Intentionally place the vacuum and listen to the music in its drone. Feel the water flowing over your hands as you swirl the dishcloth over the plates.

If busy thoughts arise, gently redirect your awareness to the experience and feel of the activity. Soon, your mind will begin to clear and settle.

Practice 3: Ground

So often, we are in the mind and disconnected from the body. When you feel like you're "all up in your head," tap your feet on the floor (or on the earth). Feel the floor supporting you—notice the texture of the wood, carpet, or grass. Feel yourself rooting back into your body. You can do this over the span of just a few breaths, or pause to ground for several minutes.

If you're at work or in a public place, you can also ground by tapping your fingers on a tabletop or the arm of a chair. Concentrate on the sensation of the wood or metal under your fingers. Bring your awareness back into the body; this will open the way for Soul.

Practice 4: My Understanding of Soul

Note: it will be helpful for you to read through this practice fully before starting.

Grab a notebook and pen. (You will be writing the questions below in your journal and leaving space for answers.)

Tap your feet on the floor (see Practice 3 above) to ground your energy and bring your awareness into your body.

With your eyes closed, take a deep belly breath in through your nose and exhale completely through your mouth. Repeat four more times.

With your fingertips, tap your heart space three times. Ask the first question from the list below. Breathe and listen, then write. Let the words flow, even if you don't fully understand them. Capture what arises. If nothing arises, that is okay, too; move on to the next question and repeat the process.

When you are complete, go about the next experience of the day. You can always add more to your notes later as thoughts or insights arise.

- "What is my understanding of Soul?"
- "How have I experienced Soul?"

If "Soul" isn't a resonant word for you, begin with this question instead: "What term describes the energy of Soul for me?" Then, return to the first question, replacing "Soul" with the word(s) of your choosing.

Becoming Soul-Aware

Two years have passed since that coaching call when Natalia surrendered to her 911.

From the outside, her life doesn't look much different. She still has her high-powered job. Her friends are still an active, treasured part of her life (and still call to share their crises). She's still the go-to resource when people in her orbit need support. On the inside, though … everything is different.

Natalia has encountered, and built a new relationship with, her Soul. And that in turn has changed how outside stressors show up for her, and how she chooses to manage them. Learning to cultivate stillness has been a game-changer for her. At first, it felt awkward and unproductive—yet, with practice, she has discovered that she actually enjoys silence. She has also noticed that creative sparks and clarity pop up with regard to whatever she is navigating or wanting to create. She has reclaimed her ability to discern, speak, and act on her truth. And while it isn't always easy, she is clear on how she wants to experience life, and sets her boundaries accordingly. She supports others with genuine love and caring, not from obligation or guilt. She is willing to act on Soul guidance even when it feels initially uncomfortable. And, when she pulled back on fixing and over-functioning, her friends and coworkers began to find their own way.

Natalia still hears the echoes of her parents' voices telling her to be available for others and not to "get too big for her britches." However, it is softer, and she quickly shifts to listening and moving from her deeper truths and wisdom. Now that she can detach with more ease from the false narrative that she needs to be everything to everybody, she allows others to be there for her. Her health is improving as she prioritizes rest, self-care, nutrition, and mindful movement. And while her marriage is still evolving, both she and her husband are committed to showing up with more transparency, compassion, and vulnerability. They are finding their "together" and both feel that they are better together today than ever before.

Most important of all, her new connection to Soul has liberated Natalia to feel fully alive and free in her life. She is living life on her terms for the first time—and, she says, "It's all *for* me, and I'm ready to receive it."

I could not have logically mapped out my life thus far.

There is something bigger going on.

Forces greater than my logical mind

guided the way and moved me

in the direction of

fulfillment, impact, and contribution.

Chapter 5

Mind

I direct my Mind in service of my Soul.

"Why isn't this working? Did I get it wrong?" James grew up in a stable, successful household. His father and mother were an engineer and a teacher, respectively. Their family was very close—and also very buttoned-up and stoic.

Around the dinner table, conversation usually focused on expectations and achievements. If James or his siblings earned anything shy of an "A" on their report cards, it would spark a conversation around, "What could you have done better? Where did you give less than your all?" Overtly and covertly, the focus—and the parental attention—was diverted to those who worked the hardest and achieved the most.

Prepare for the future. Have a goal—and don't stop until you achieve it. Be relentless in your pursuit of excellence.

These were the themes that ruled James's life.

Despite his straight-A report cards and numerous awards in sports and academics, James never saw himself as "enough." He watched friends and peers whom he perceived to be smarter, more successful, and more secure financially, and used their achievements as a goad to push himself to greater and greater heights. "Discipline and control" was his mantra—and denying his emotions was part of that protocol. Whether he was getting roughed up on the football field, feeling frustrated, dealing with a painful breakup, or just noticing tension in a room, he brushed it all aside. Getting emotional meant he was out of control, and lack of control was a sign of weakness.

Post-college, James created and put in play a well-formulated plan to create the success, freedom, and exceptional quality of life he envisioned. He experienced progressive success early in his career, thanks in large part to his discipline and constant pursuit of growth. However, despite this, he never learned to check out of work and actually enjoy the life he'd created. Unplugging was not in his mile-long list of skills. In fact, the more he had to do, the harder he dove in. He told himself and his family that he would come up for air when the business slowed down, but it never did. There was always something unfinished—something that mattered a great deal to the business's performance, his reputation, and of course the rewards of his income, stocks, and benefits.

From the outside, James's tactics seemed to be working. He had an amazing life, a beautiful home, and a loving family. Yes, he worked hard, and was often exhausted ... but it was worth it when you considered the big picture, right?

Well, maybe.

Each night, James carefully reviewed his day to look for opportunities for improvement—just as he had done as a child at his parents' dinner table. Anything shy of excellence was, in his mind, a failure. He reviewed every interaction, every meeting. Did he choose his words and actions with care and deliberation? Did he make the right decisions?

James thought it was helping him to do these nightly reviews. He thought that rehearsing his interactions safeguarded him from making mistakes. But with his mind running the show, his Soul had no chance to be heard. He was locked in a vicious cycle of "analysis paralysis" and overthinking, which was making it impossible for him to enjoy the life he'd worked so hard to build.

His 911 came in the form of a "perfect storm" of global and personal events. The Covid-19 pandemic significantly impacted his business. His year-end goals wouldn't come close to being met. At the same time, the stock market crashed. His well-planned, carefully-managed retirement portfolio was now set back by years.

His mind went wild, thinking, *How bad will this get? What if the market doesn't rebound?* The more out of control he felt, the more he engaged in repetitive scenario-planning. It was exhausting. Burdensome. He felt immense pressure because, in his mind, it was all up to him. He *had* to fix this before it got even worse.

The trouble was, he couldn't seem to think his way out of

this. His mind would get clear on one direction, only to argue the opposite strategy an hour later. Soon, it began to feel like *nothing* was within his control. "Why is this not working?" he asked himself over and over. "It always has before!"

While all this was unfolding, James also went from traveling three weeks a month to being on total lockdown. Pre-pandemic, he'd seen himself as close with his family—a frequently-absent, yet supportive and beloved, provider. Now, at home full-time with his wife and teenage daughter, he felt like a stranger in his own home. He had missed so much over the years. Not the big things—he deliberately planned his schedule around events like graduations, recitals, and birthdays—rather, the little things. The daily happenings with his daughter's friends. His wife's new passion for drawing. The inside jokes and banter that he couldn't keep up with, and the references to memories he hadn't been a part of. While he was building his meticulously constructed "path to freedom," had he missed out on what truly mattered?

It all came to a head when James's wife found a lump in her breast. What if he had traded away his best years with her for his career? Would he be able to live with himself?

He had meant well. He had operated from the belief that if he firmly secured their future, he and his family would be able to do whatever they wanted—that they would have all the time in the world.

His self-attacking thoughts would not relent. *Did I get it wrong?*

Each day, James awoke feeling guilty, anxious, and uptight.

He felt like he was about to implode—and yet, implosion would have gone totally against his vision of himself as a paragon of control. He felt like he couldn't let his wife and daughter see that, just under the surface, it was all falling apart. That *he* was falling apart.

So, he did what he usually did: he got busy. Only this time, it didn't work. His regret and fear were deafening. Everything he thought he knew, everything he had spent his life building and planning for, was being called into question, and he no longer had the answers.

This is where James was when we met for our first session. Immediately, it was clear that his challenge wasn't control, accountability, stability, or success. It wasn't his work ethic, or his ability to deliver results. Nor was it a lack of love and devotion for his family.

It was his relationship to Mind.

What *is* Mind?

The mind at its best is a powerful tool for navigating life with ease and joy. It's an ally in realizing our greatest joy, potential, meaning, and impact. It allows us to experience and draw information from multiple states and places at the same time—something that no other creature on Earth (that we know of) can do.

The mind at its worst is a menacing and self-punishing deterrent that cements and perpetuates negative states like inaction, fear, frustration, and lack. Under the auspices of "control" and "protection," it invokes repetitive, obstructive thoughts, feelings, and actions that keep recreating a familiar past in the present, which sets the stage for a future that is vastly different than what we desire.

Perhaps you've experienced that particular whiplash of a mind gone wild. The flip-flopping between stories of what is and what can (and cannot) be. The giddy anticipation and igniting momentum suddenly sabotaged by overwhelm, uncertainty, and loss. The utter obliteration of confidence by a few sneaky thoughts, followed by a retreat into familiar patterns of settling, avoiding, running, or numbing. And the way that all of this unfolds under a placid surface until something comes along to shake things up—like a Soul 911.

Mind is not your enemy. It's not an unproductive hamster wheel of chatter that keeps you stuck, overwhelmed, and feeling like crap. Nevertheless, you can *experience* Mind that way until you understand how to use it as the tool it is—a tool in service to Soul.

Oh, I get it. If someone had told me in the middle of my own 911 that I should use my mind in service to Soul, I would have raised my eyebrows, smiled vaguely, and instantly returned to whatever frenetic, scenario-laden train of thought I was immersed in. Now, I see things differently—as you can when you come out of the Earth View of Mind and into the Soul View.

THE EARTH VIEW OF MIND

The story you tell yourself is powerful. Often the one you tell yourself the most is the one you make come true.

It's likely that you've heard this adage in some form. "Thoughts become things." Or this one: "If you think you can, or you think you can't, you're right."

And, you've also likely thought, *If it were that simple, I would already have everything I want. I think about what I want all the time, and yet it isn't so. What gives?*

The issue isn't that we don't think about what we desire. It's that we *also* allow ourselves to get strapped in for a roller-coaster ride of other, unproductive thoughts that steer us in the exact opposite direction of the experiences we desire.

Thoughts turn into stories—and we tell *a lot* of stories about ourselves, about other people, and about the world. About what is possible and what is not. About what we can have and what we can't. The challenge is that, often, these stories are inaccurate; sometimes, they're outright fiction.

As the Buddhist teacher, Tara Brach, shared: "Our thoughts are real, but they are not *reality*."

In the Earth View of Mind, we operate in daily life from the conditioned self—meaning, the learned *false self* of personality and ego—versus the True Self, which is Soul. Your conditioned self is created over the course of your lifetime from thoughts, feelings, ideas, perceptions, and beliefs related to your lived experiences. From an early age, you made meaning from your experiences and you developed compensatory coping strategies of habits (i.e., perfectionism, playing small) and roles (i.e., people pleaser, over-achiever) out of protection and to solve for unmet needs, wounds, or fears.

Layer upon layer of stories and beliefs combined to inform

who you have become. The sources contributing to perception of self are vast. Earth Tribe influences—including key events, experiences, patterns, and thought forms from the community we live in and hang out with, as well as the collective mind—and Soul Tribe influences—like our parents/guardians, gestation experience, past/parallel lives, as well as the universal mind: all contribute to the whole that is "who we are," or rather, who we *perceive* ourselves to be. Imagine if you were raised in another state or country, with different parental and community influences. How different would your life be right now?

Some of the layers of stories and beliefs imparted by our Earth Tribe and Soul Tribe influences are empowering. Many are not. Most are double-edged, and can either help or hinder us depending on the expression that Soul is calling us toward.

For example, James's planning, analysis, and willingness to always do better served him extraordinarily well in his career. However, there came a time when these patterns no longer served him—when, in fact, they were preventing him from opening to the gift that Soul was offering. Instead of prompting, "Do more," Soul was inviting him to say, "I am enough."

I've worked with thousands of clients who share the limiting belief of *I am not enough*. Rarely does someone literally say those words; rather the belief plays out as an undercurrent. They might see themselves as too tall, too short, too thin, too wide. Too little hair. Too much nose. Not enough money. Not the right house, the right car, the right parents, the right connections. Maybe they feel like they can never do enough to earn that A+ grade or get that dream promotion. For James, this played out in his constant planning and rehearsing of scenarios. Subconsciously, he believed that *he wasn't enough.* He planned for every scenario and tried to control every aspect of life because, deep inside, he feared that he wasn't capable of meeting the next set of challenges. He held to that pattern until Soul stepped in with his 911.

Other common limiting beliefs play out across a spectrum of experiences. Some of the ones I see most are: *I have to give to be loved. Money is hard to come by. The world isn't safe for me.* These may *feel* real—especially if we have experienced trauma during our time here on Earth,—yet they are still, at their core, beliefs.

Marissa Peer summed it up well in her powerful quote: "First, you make your beliefs, and then your beliefs make you."

The Earth View of Mind is that Mind is supreme. Mind is informed by physicality, the five senses, and the conditioned self. Fear is its fuel. When put in charge without checks and balances, Mind will create feelings of overwhelm, separation, anger, jealousy, superiority, inferiority, and desire for power based on perceived lack. Why is this so? Because Mind's job is to solve problems and keep us safe.

In this view, *we see what we look for.* We see our interpretation of situations and events. We see other people through our filters and stories. When we aren't aware of them, these (often skewed) perceptions are entrenched and unlikely to change, even when we are presented with strong evidence to the contrary. And when story meets story, which happens daily in all forms of communication between people, both parties bring assumption, assignment of meaning, biased perception, and judgment to bear. This dialogue of story (both spoken and unspoken) often impedes open, effective communication.

When steeped in Earth View, Mind looks to the material world to scan for answers. These answers are often recycled, limited, or inherently biased. When you feel "wound up," it's likely that Mind is offering an incessant stream of fear-based chatter. Aware that you feel in need of protection, it makes you aware of everything that could go wrong.

This is why Mind can be such a potent source of suffering. Often, I'll hear clients being incredibly hard on themselves. Maybe you have been hard on yourself, too, thinking things like, "I should be happy. People want my life." Or, "I should have seen this coming. What will people think about me?" Or, "What have I done to deserve this?" Fear-based thoughts can be brutal. But Mind, alone, always brings us back to those places, because that is where we are conditioned to dwell.

This goes beyond just the personal. Because our society at large is led by Mind, much of the material world is configured in fear. We focus on what is breaking down—whether that be in media, politics, medicine, or social justice issues. In an attempt to avoid looming danger, we succumb to judgments and division. We make our beliefs and stories about other groups of people true—because this "truth" lends us a measure of certainty when all else feels uncertain.

Despite its drawbacks, Mind is actually an amazing tool for

shaping, amplifying, and sorting experiences and information. It can be a creative generator. Though all of us have experienced patterns of Mind that are disruptive, limiting, or painful, Mind is infinitely changeable, and can, if you allow it, be guided and pointed by Soul. This is where things get exciting.

Whether you are experiencing an urgent 911 or your 911 has been percolating for years, it's vital to think beyond what your mind (fueled by the conditioned self) currently believes is possible, and allow your Soul to step in as a guide. If you are not experiencing a 911, now is still a perfect time to explore the expanded capacity and capability available when you transition into the Soul View of Mind.

THE SOUL VIEW OF MIND

Soul knows that everything that is held in the universal mind— Source, God, the Quantum, or whatever idea you resonate with is available to you. It understands the architecture of the universe and the expansive playground of possibilities that are waiting for you to explore.

Teresa of Avila was reported to have said, "Your mind can't make the journey." The rational mind simply cannot make sense of the great mystery of life. It operates from the material, not the mystical; from the proven, not the unknown. The ways in which we normally walk through the day—attached to thoughts, repeating "what if" scenarios, micromanaging our actions, striving for control, racing against the clock—limit access to and awareness of higher states of consciousness.

The irony is, we must lose the mind as we know it to transcend our self-imposed limitations.

The unchecked mind dwells in what is humanly possible according to our current beliefs and experiences. The Soul dwells in what is infinitely possible. The higher purpose of Mind, then, is to enliven the vast potentiality of Soul and make Soul's desire manifest in material reality.

From the expansive Soul View, you are *awareness*.

You, as awareness, become the witness of your thoughts. You know you are not your thoughts. They don't have to mean a thing; you can choose to ignore them. If you have a totally nutty thought (like, "What if squirrels were green?"), you can easily dismiss it as nonsense. Similarly, as awareness, you can note the feelings generated by Mind's thoughts and be playful with them. *Who is anxious? Oh, yes, that's my false self/Earth View Mind dipping into fear again!* This distinction between who you are and what you think about allows you to anchor in your True Self, where you can honor and tend to the feelings without letting them take control (versus getting carried away by your thoughts and feelings).

In the Soul View, Mind is informed and engaged with solving for solutions through creative vision. It sees beyond the problem at hand to a greater geography of potentialities. Instead of working at the level of the problem, Soul-led Mind works at the level of possibility.

In the same way, from the Soul View of Mind, you can take direction from your higher intelligence and dismiss thoughts that are born from fear and limiting beliefs. Soul knows that not *all* thoughts become things. Only when you allow fearful thoughts to take over the truth of your vibration can they shift your reality to match. For example, I've had clients who have had periodic thoughts of financial disarray for years, but financial struggle was never one of their lessons in life. Though their thoughts caused temporary distress, the greater truth (and the majority of their thoughts) were of financial security. Fear-based thoughts will cross your radar, as you are learning to live more consistently from the Soul View of Mind, but *predominant felt experience* is the key for vibration and creation.

It may seem as though, in Soul View, the conditioned mind is banished or negated. That isn't the case. In fact, the work of Soul-led Mind is to integrate and love the protective, scared, and anxious parts of yourself. When you invite the conditioned mind to step into the ocean of awareness that is Soul, what you will discover is *consciousness*.

Here, love is the fuel. Compassion, understanding, harmony, connection, support, and power for greater good all become available. Expansive views become common. Judgments evaporate. Problems and obstacles become Earth School lessons to engage with and learn from.

From the Soul View of Mind, you have access to information that is beyond the physical. We touched on this in Chapter 4, but now, we'll make it specific to Mind.

The following questions related to the expanded capabilities of Mind are excerpted from Marcus Anthony's "Discover Your Soul" template. I find Marcus's approach to be among the most aligned and robust for working with Mind in this way.

Place a check mark next to any of the following that you have experienced.

    _   I have sensed what will happen in the future.

    _   I have known things and/or people without being told about them.

    _   I have sensed where things were without prior knowledge of their location.

    _   I have the ability to intuitively find the causes of problems.

    _   I sense connections between seemingly unrelated things.

    _   I intuitively determine the value or wisdom of different choices.

    _   I get creative knowledge and ideas from spiritual sources.

    _   Information comes to me spontaneously; sometimes, I "just know."

    _   I sometimes see things and events before they manifest physically.

    _   I hear messages like they are being spoken.

    _   I feel and sense the emotions of people, animals, plants, or spirits.*

Chances are, you have had at least one of the above experiences in your lifetime.

---

* *Anthony, Marcus. 2012. Discover Your Soul Template. Rochester, Vermont.*

These types of occurrences are also known as:

- *Foresense*: Sensing what is going to happen in the future.*

- *Integrated recognition: Knowing somebody or something without ever being told about them.*

- *Integrated location: Capacity to sense where things are without having prior knowledge.*

- *Integrated diagnosis: Ability to intuitively find the cause of problems.*

- *Integrated connection: Sensing connection between and among things.*

- *Integrated evaluation: Intuitively determining the wisdom or value of different options.*

- *Inspiration**: Creative knowledge and ideas that come from spiritual sources, not the conscious/conditioned mind.*

- *Claircognizance (clear knowing): Information that comes to you spontaneously that you "just know."*

- *Clairvoyance (clear seeing): Seeing things that actually manifest physically.*

- *Clairaudience (clear hearing): Perceiving or hearing sounds or messages either audibly or inside your mind.*

- *Clairsentience (clear feeling) Feeling and sensing emotions of people, animals, or spirits.*

---

* through **: Anthony, Marcus. 2012. Discover Your Soul Template. Rochester, Vermont.

Have you ever heard yourself say, "I knew something was off!" or, "I had a feeling that was going to happen"? You had an experience of nonphysical awareness.

Same goes if you've ever sensed that, although someone's words were telling you, "All is well," something just felt "off." Maybe the feeling in your body was heavy or anxious, or you just knew something wasn't adding up. Later, you discovered that the person was indeed upset about something, but they weren't ready to talk about it. Your sense of incongruence was a direct result of your connection to the expansive aspects of Mind.

For years, I purposefully shut down many of my intuitive gifts. They just didn't seem to jive with the "executive" vibe. Unless I could back up an assertion with a business case or other facts, I held back my voice. Later, of course, I would find out that what I sensed was spot on. I often wondered how my intuition would have been received if I had given voice to it at the time; I suspect not well. Even today, while many business leaders are starting to embrace the value of "instincts," my clients report that facts and established data are sovereign, and "hunches" or "gut feelings"—let alone clairsentience or claircognizance—are met with skepticism or brushed aside entirely.

It's time for the "and."

THE BEAUTY OF THE "AND"

"Exhausted. Stuck. Anxious. Like my world is on fire and I have no water to put it out."

That is how James described how he was feeling on our first call. He was perplexed that his formerly reliable brain simply could not figure out the best path forward. And now, wracked with guilt over his family, it was even harder to think clearly and stop the barrage of attacking thoughts. He wanted to feel at peace with his choices around family and work, and obtain support on how to navigate these unfamiliar waters.

A mind that plays a disempowered story on repeat will not *allow* you to feel at peace or free, no matter how much success or time or vitality you have. However, when Mind is anchored in love, empowered by vision and imagination, and aligned with the knowing of Soul ... that, my friend, is the way to freedom. More, it is a call to live as you were meant to live—as a fully sovereign being.

Does a mind in service to Soul mean you also live free from stress and pain? Although you may wish for that in moments, the answer is, most likely, no. You came here to be human, and to learn and grow. Change is part of the package and propels you out of the nest so you can embrace your power and fly.

In James's case, as with all 911s, there was a greater invitation masked in the details of his crisis.

I often say, "Your body's truth precedes your mind's lies." Meaning, when you're stuck in the mind-swirl, you get disconnected from your body and the deeper truths of Soul and universal intelligence. Your body often sends signals that something is off-course long before the onset of your 911. That was true for James, too. Before the "perfect storm," he experienced many restless nights, disturbed by thoughts that his balance in life was off. However, only when things unraveled did he pause to reevaluate.

It's essential to note the swirling as it arises and attune inward so Soul's wisdom can be revealed. Once that wisdom is clear, Mind becomes a vehicle for higher action. You can make plans, set goals, and execute strategies in service to Soul wisdom. Mind is now a partner, rather than an enemy. More, you have a vast capacity to leverage Soul's clarity to evolve who you are *being,* and how you show up in life and in service.

Reimagining your relationship to Mind is an invitation to rise above and see beyond your current conditions—beyond what seems realistic, or even possible—and allow yourself to play in the space of possibility. This also means reimagining what your 911 is actually about. When you create space and anchor in the expanded intelligence of Heart (more to come about this in the Heart chapter), Soul will inform you how to move through and thrive beyond the uncertainty and discomfort you're experiencing. You may receive insight and clarity on protective habits or roles that now require fine-tuning, or about old, lingering stories and beliefs that are ready to be transfigured and replaced with new versions that reflect and support the real you. There's always a reveal seeking light—a birth, a renewal, or a release.

Even if it seems limiting circumstances are playing out in your life right now, in front of you is a big, clear canvas of unlimited possibility. Remember, the stories you're telling yourself right now are just that: stories. If you can step back into that space of *being the awareness*, another layer of clarity will emerge, and the seedlings of direction, inspiration, peace (or whatever you seek) will be planted in the fertile soil of Soul. Then, you can step back into your current reality and set your Mind to the task for which is it eminently suited: constructing a future guided by Soul.

Living in the beauty of the "and" means not making Mind the enemy, but rather navigating its gifts with intention and love. When storms of thoughts from the conditioned self are thrashing about, send them some love, and bless them. Mind likes to be in charge—yet only when Mind is informed, aligned, and fueled by Soul is what you seek made clear and possible.

Working *with* Mind

The Center for Computational Biology at the University of Southern California estimates that we each think approximately 70,000 thoughts a day. Most of those are thoughts we've had before, and will have again, over and over until something changes.

I bucket our thoughts into two overarching categories: Love or Fear. Where you invest your thought energy significantly influences what you experience in life and how you experience it.

Here's how that plays out.

Contained within those 70,000 thoughts are a bunch of words. Words in a song that transport you back to a cherished memory or bring tears to your eyes. Words uttered by someone you respect that ignited your belief and inspired you to take action. Words spoken by yourself or others that instantaneously shattered the confidence you felt only moments before. Words you spoke while looking into a mirror that sabotaged your biggest dreams or empowered you for liftoff.

Words turn into thoughts. Thoughts (including automatic thoughts, visual images, beliefs, and memories) turn into stories that inform how you feel and what choices you make. Thoughts, feelings, and actions influence the vibration you emit. (Yes, "vibration" is a real thing. Your body creates its own electromagnetic field which vibrates at the frequency created by, among other things, your thoughts and feelings.) Your vibration in turn influences your results and life experiences because it determines what energies you attract and repel.

The simplified formula looks like this. It is both linear and circular.

Thoughts + Feelings → Behavior → Vibration = Result/Life Experience

The more you repeat your thoughts and words, the more deeply they are felt. Evidence suggests that your words—whether thought silently or spoken out loud—ultimately impact the wiring in your brain, your biology, even your DNA expression.

In the powerful book, *Words Can Change Your Brain*, physician Andrew Newberg, M.D. and co-author Mark Waldman state: "A single word has the power to influence the expression of genes that regulate physical and emotional stress."

For all its brilliance, Mind directs your body and behaviors in a manner that is predominantly subconscious. In fact, leading researcher Dr. Bruce Lipton asserts that we operate from our subconscious mind 95 percent of the time, and from our creative conscious mind only 5 percent of the time. You can probably think of a time when you got in your car, started driving, and then reached your destination with no memory of how you got there. It's the same concept; we're all on autopilot a great deal of the time.

After we repeat something enough times, the mind no longer has to consciously manage it; the body simply takes over. Sometimes, this is benign—like brushing your teeth or making your morning coffee. Other times, we are engaging in crucial life activities without ever realizing that we're playing out our subconscious beliefs and deep-rooted stories. This is how someone like James—a hardworking, intelligent, talented individual—could diligently apply himself in the name of "freedom, someday" and yet create the opposite. During the times of the day when he was on autopilot, his belief of "not enough" was running the show, and creating his experience accordingly.

Complicating matters further is the fact that we don't just have one brain. Researchers have identified three distinct neural networks (read: brains) in the head, heart, and gut. Each of these have their own unique nervous systems, and can independently process and store information. Our three "brains" are connected by the vagus nerve, which functions like an information "highway."*

---

https://spinalresearch.com.au/three-brains-head-heart-gut-sometimes-conflict

The three brains have distinct roles.

- **Head:** Analytical/cognitive thinking, perception, language, narratives, cognition, recognition.
- **Heart:** Emotional/affective, processing emotions, values.
- **Gut:** Intuition, safety/protection, self-preservation, processing fear, anxiety, mobility, action, key immune functions.

70 to 80 percent of the information we receive flows up the vagal channel to the "head brain," not the other way around. By the time we can clearly think about a feeling or reaction, it's already been processed. This is why, when you sense danger in your gut or hear your Heart wisdom, it's hard at times to talk your head into listening and acting upon it—particularly when there's no visible proof to back it up. It's fascinating to observe this dynamic within ourselves, particularly when we've been taught that the brain is the sole source of intelligence in the body.*

Mind is a powerful tool, however there is a higher intelligence and consciousness to access in the Heart. The Heart, not the brain, is the gateway to the universal mind.

It comes down to this: the mind, especially when operating in Earth View, is not as trustworthy or objective as we have been led to believe. It doesn't operate in isolation, and it doesn't always offer accurate perceptions because it can't distinguish what is real from what is imagination.

---

*https://spinalresearch.com.au/three-brains-head-heart-gut-sometimes-conflict

As an example, I offer a view of my own inner nuttiness during the middle of my 911, when I was trying to decide whether to stay on my corporate path or take the leap into the unknown.

Back and forth, back and forth my thoughts went. My imagination ran wild with dreams of living with more freedom. Dreams of having more time with my children, family, and friends. Dreams of writing a book, speaking on large stages, and impacting millions of lives. Dreams of feeling like my life had a deep meaning and purpose.

Yes, I thought. *This is what I want. It's so clear. My decision is made.*

Then … boom! Mind kicked in with every worst-case scenario I could conjure up. *You're setting yourself up for ruin. Why would you choose that? How could you be that selfish?*

I applied my prior therapy strategies to neutralize the thought stream. *What if it wasn't ruin? What if it was opportunity?*

Fine, maybe not ruin, my argumentative mind replied. *But why can't you just be? You love your job and the opportunities it offers. Why take a chance and jeopardize what's working so well? You've got no fallback, punkin. Single mom, sole breadwinner … and you like shoes. You like shoes a lot. And travel. And handbags. Why put all that stuff at risk?*

Yet, something inside me kept calling me forward. *There's more for you, and through you. Be brave. Trust yourself.*

Trust life.

My heart and gut brains said "GO!" even though my head didn't have the evidence to support my choice. I had to override the whiplash of fear to move into a new, more fully expanded way of being. I had to move from fear thoughts to love-based thoughts. Most of all, I had to choose to align with the whispers to leave (which I now know were Heart and Soul-informed) in order to discern greater truths, possibilities, and the path forward. I can see clearly now that I was activating Mind in service to Soul. The leap into the unknown was the beginning of coming to remember who I was, what I could become, and why I was seeking to embody my True Self.

We often live up to what we've been told we are capable of. The voices of our early caregivers, significant influences, and even society tell us what we are capable of, and what is humanly possible. These voices are often laden with fear, limited by experience, and proven by perception. Even an optimistic Earth View is often artificially restricted in terms of possibility and scope.

By remaining in Earth View around a 911, we deny our Soul's knowing and the greatest possibilities for our lives. So, if your mind has talked you away from (or completely out of) the very things you're yearning for, know that you are being called back to Soul View. You are receiving an invitation to remember and activate the divine creator being within and access the Mind field beyond all your current stories and perceptions.

Nature and the Mind

Nature plays a unique role in Mind, by virtue of having the power to slow or even shut off the thought stream that prevents us from accessing Soul wisdom.

The Earth is our first mother, and she is in relationship with us daily—even when life, work, family, finances, and screens of all sizes distract us. She is in constant communication with us.

One of the most potent ways to engage Mind from Soul View is to interact with nature. Take time to walk on the Earth with deliberate intention. Notice what you notice. Within everything that catches your eye, there is a message of love and support, if you are willing to receive it. That leaf falling gently in front of you is a reminder to let go with grace. The sun peeking through the trees to touch your face is an invitation to be the light. The birdsong outside your window is a personal chorus to raise your spirits. Endless messages offer endless chances to reflect and still the mental chatter. The more present you are, the easier it will be to receive these transmissions.

Each time I immerse myself in nature, I receive the messages I most need to hear. Every. Single. Time. And you will, too.

So, if your mind won't stop, take a moment to lie on your back and gaze at the stars. Lose your mind in the boundless sky and see what happens. Listen, and look. Breathe in the majesty of it all. Feel your childlike wonder ignite. Allow the expansiveness to paint new possibility and weave it into the story you want to author—the one that makes you feel fully alive and free.

It's all there for you.

Practices

Below are multiple practices to help you reflect on how you told the story of your 911, settle a busy brain, and shift from the Earth View of Mind to activate a greater field of possibility via Soul.

Beyond the Reflect practice, choose whichever practices you need in this moment (i.e., Settle, Shift, or Expand) and come back to the rest in future days.

REFLECT

Awareness of *how* you tell the story of your 911 (to yourself and to others) is super important. Take a spin and reread the story you captured in Chapter 3.

- What stands out to you?
- What do you tend to amplify and how does that make you feel?
- What is one love-based shift you are willing to introduce (even if you don't yet believe it) in how you tell the story?

SETTLE AND SHIFT

Hum

Humming has many benefits ranging from vocal strategy to powerful spiritual practice. It's also a very effective, easy way to calm the mind, as it creates balance between parasympathetic and sympathetic response.

- Gently touch your lips together with teeth apart.

- Relax your jaw.

- Close your eyes and breathe in deeply. On your exhale, create a "mmm" sound without opening your lips.

- Continue to hum through your exhale. Feel the vibration in your face.

- Engage in the rhythm of breathing in and humming on the exhale for between 30 seconds and two minutes.

Helpful hint: if you are out in public, you can hum to a tune; otherwise, a single tone is good.

Honor and Release with Tapping

Sometimes you just want to get out of the mental swirl.

The combination of speaking your 911 story out loud while engaging in a modified Emotional Freedom Tapping (EFT) technique will help to move the energy and emotions trapped in your body. (Note: if you'd like to view the complete process of Tapping, there are a plethora of full EFT demonstrations on YouTube. The Tapping Solution is one good starting place).

My clients consistently report the modified EFT version below works great for them. It's easy to use when at work (provided you find a quiet, private space where you can speak aloud), in the car, or on a walk. For this version, you only tap on the collarbone or on the side of your hand (karate chop).

Abbreviated Tapping Technique

- Tap on your collarbone while speaking what you are thinking out loud. Whatever the worry, fear or feelings that are distressing you, give them voice. (It's just like talking out loud describing a stressor to a friend, only this time you speak it out loud for yourself while tapping.)

- After a few minutes of speaking and tapping, pause and breathe.

- If you feel like you need another round to get it all out, do so. (Note: I recommend keeping this part of the process to a few minutes.) When you're done, pause and breathe again.

- Now, tap on your collarbone while speaking a generative possibility. Think of how you would encourage someone you love, and speak that to yourself. For example, you might say, *I've got this. I never travel alone. I've made it through tough stuff before. Somehow, I always get through—and I know I will this time, too. I am open to all available support. I choose to align with my highest wisdom and path, and look forward to creative solutions, and new possibilities. It's safe to relax.*

- Repeat this for up to five minutes, always ending on generative possibility.

Grounding Breathwork & Shift to Love

- Ground your feet on the earth. Be barefoot if possible.

- Breathe in through your nose, really feeling the breath expand your tummy and lungs. Exhale completely through your mouth, making the exhale longer than your inhale. Do this with your eyes closed. If that's not possible, blink your eyes a few times while you breathe.

- Tap your heart space/collarbone (or underside of a table if with others) to move your attention back into your body.

- Ask one of these questions to move your energy from fear into love:
  - What would Love do?
  - What is my *one* next best action?
  - What is one higher thought that I can embrace right now?

- Take one small action to move forward in a positive way.

EXPAND

Expand Your Senses

As you animate your five senses, you begin to ignite untapped, expanded sensory capabilities.

It's ideal to experience this practice outside in nature. However, if this isn't possible, you can engage with it in your home. Go through each sense, activating one at a time. Have fun, and enjoy the sense of calm, creativity, and connectedness that follows!

- *What do you see?* Pick one thing you see and really explore it. What colors do you see? Is it moving, still or swaying? What patterns do you see in the object? Is it big or small, wide or long?

- *What do you hear?* Pause and listen. What sounds do you hear? Are they pleasing? Soft or loud? Is there any rhythm or cadence you notice?

- *What do you smell?* You can stay with the same object or walk a little further and notice something else. Really breathe in, picking up any scents around you. Is the air fresh? Perhaps you scent an animal nearby, or fresh-cut grass. If your sense of smell is not high, think about what it might smell like. Make it up.

- *Touch an object.* How does it feel? Sticky, sharp, rigid, soft or something else? Are there any smooth edges? Is it bigger or smaller than you? Is it solid or hollow?

- *Taste something.* If you are outside, imagine tasting water from a fresh spring meadow or a crisp apple from a tree. If you are inside, imagine tasting a fresh baked lemon pie, cold, creamy vanilla ice cream, or a piece of sushi. Get creative: what would that flower taste like?

When all of your senses have been engaged, rest in the expansion. Just breathe. Be. See what emerges now or later in the day.

Becoming Mind-Aware

By the time James reached out for coaching, he was open to testing and trying whatever might help him navigate his overwhelming stress and worry.

When we reflected on the story he was telling about his 911, he was able to observe the false self and how steeped it was in untenable fear. He recognized that he had lost sight of the bigger picture and his invested energy did not necessarily line up with his highest priorities. Our open dialogue about his fear that he had lost time with his wife and kids helped him discern his limiting stories and beliefs.

When he learned to settle his mind and tune into Soul View, it opened a whole new expanded perspective. Now, when he notes his conditioned self predicting overwhelm and impossibility, he gets playful rather than controlling. "Is this my 5:00 a.m. false self, or my superpowered self?" he asks. This shift was huge for him.

James reports with great joy that he now creates quality time with his children and wife. They engage in weekly and monthly family experiences that he treasures—and during them, he is fully present. His wife's cancer scare did not materialize, and they are thriving.

At work, he has released unfounded assumptions that

everything is up to him and now invites others into his problem solving. In doing so, he has freed up capacity for creative time, and solutions arise with far greater ease.

When he feels wound up, his go-to practice is Tapping. Coming up with the generative statements was foreign at first, as he'd been filled with self-attacking thoughts for so long. However, when he spoke out loud what he would say to a friend (despite not believing it at first), he started to see himself in a new light. More, he has been able to generate acceptance of his past decisions, keep the habits and roles that still serve him and others, and let the rest go with love.

We all do the best we can at any given time. The fear-based mind serves no one. Self-punishment, worry, and fear create a kind of hell on Earth. Of course, in hindsight, there are decisions we would make differently; these are not calls to berate ourselves, but rather to reflect, learn, adapt, and begin again. With each iteration, we become wiser and more loving. Each time we choose to direct Mind in service to Soul, we claim the most powerful gifts on offer from life.

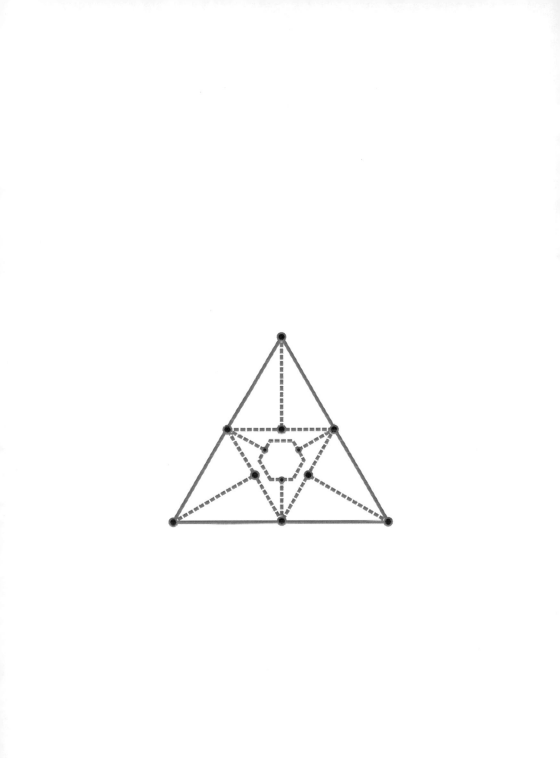

Settle in.

Rest and Renew.

A wondrous universe of infinite possibility awaits.

Vast vistas beaming with beauty.

Adventure and love beyond imagination.

All for you.

Right here within this miraculous suit called Body.

Chapter 6

I honor my Body as the vehicle of my Soul.

Like most of us, I've put some hard miles on my body. Years of overly jammed days as an executive. Back-to-back meetings. Constant time-zone hopscotch. The endless to-do lists. Trying to be the best possible mom. Juggling competing personal and business demands. Being over-available to anyone in need. Operating on so little sleep that it was a wonder I didn't fall face-first into my laptop. It was a cycle of neglect and lack of connection with my physical self that I wasn't even fully aware of. While I exercised often and ate healthily, that couldn't make up for the lack of rest and renewal. "Work hard, play hard" was my motto. I pushed my body to unhealthy limits yet hoped it would continue to thrive. It was an unsustainable ask of my one and only vessel.

When the busyness stopped in my business (and I finally

restored a sleep routine), I moved into a more subtle (but still very real) betrayal of my body by tamping down my inner knowing and the feelings that arose from within my body in response to life.

Hiding out is stressful to the system. The fear of not-enoughness and anticipated judgment was far more stress-inducing than jumping out of a plane. Yet unlike skydiving, sailing the expansive canvas of the limitless sky and touching down quickly with a safe landing and ending, the fear-based chatter was a seemingly endless freefall. The more I listened to the inner critic tirades, the more I chose the "safe" route of playing small for my own protection. Inadvertently, this created an even bigger toll on my body.

There are a million little ways that your body speaks to you, saying, *Knock it off! Rest! Play! Take a freaking break!* Still, we don't often listen to these little messages, so they join forces and turn into big ones. Maybe you get a cold, or the flu. Maybe your adrenals finally say, "Enough, already!" Or maybe the symptoms are even more significant.

Although I am healthy and thriving today, and my body always looked healthy to others, I didn't get away with this betrayal of my physical vessel. Severe gastrointestinal issues, tight shoulders, feeling wound up, an inability to sleep through the night even when I had a whole night to relax … these were symptom messengers. My body wanted me to listen, and on *some* level I did. I became hypervigilant, limiting my food intake to avoid an accident. I occasionally got a massage to help manage my discomfort. Other than that, self-care was very light, and mitigating strategies took center stage.

Turns out half-listening to your body does not work any better than ignoring it does.

Along my journey, I came to understand that anything left unaddressed at an emotional or spiritual level will eventually translate into physical symptoms. The deeper message my body was mirroring to me was that *I wasn't digesting and processing life*. I was out of harmony with the dynamic exchange of giving and receiving. The symptoms reflected the lack of integrity and congruity of my choices. I now know that my over-functioning and over-availability for others was compensatory; I wanted to feel comfortable in my own skin, and desired to be seen and valued as I was. As I began to slow down, tune in, process the hidden beliefs and emotions, and live with more congruence, the symptoms resolved. They haven't returned.

The healing process wasn't instantaneous, and it wasn't easy. I had to mindfully gather and integrate all of the dispersed and scattered pieces of my energy. I had to develop the art of setting healthy boundaries. I had to bravely claim who I truly was, instead of being who I thought others needed me to be.

By sending me signals of discomfort and dis-ease, my body was doing its job—or, at least, trying to, and without much help from me. It was working to restore and repair itself, as it is coded to do. It was trying to reinstitute balance and harmony, as it is designed to. Yet, I was constantly overriding its signals, and the only way for it to get my attention and enlist my cooperation was heightened dis-ease.

Only through yoga and reiki did I come to understand how

disconnected—how *disembodied*—I was. I was living in my head, focused on some future destination, not connected at all to the two-legged miracle that is home to my Soul in this life-time. I had woefully underestimated this great ally that repeat-edly moved me in the direction of my dreams while I ignored it, mistreated it, and actively worked against it.

How was it possible that, with all my education and cre-dentials, and more than a decade of personal and professional experience in the healthcare field, I had absolutely no clue about how to listen to and work with this crazy, amazing body?

What *is* Body?

No one wakes up and says, "Today, I will abuse and take for granted my body." It's much more unconscious than that. Yet, we do mistreat our bodies—and often justify our actions as expedient in the moment. We make excuses for our neglect in the name of accomplishing goals, tasks, and obligations.

When we understand what the body is capable of, and the central role it plays on our behalf in this lifetime, we can no longer see it as separate from Mind and Soul, or as something to be dismissed. It is the singular relationship in our life—the only relationship that has been with us since conception and will be with us until we die. Neither parents, nor children, nor lovers, nor jobs, nor anything else will escort us through life from start to finish, 24/7, without exception.

So why do so many of us have such a fraught relationship (or worse, no relationship at all) with our bodies?

As I've shared, I was not a very good partner to my body for a long time. I was inconsistent, and at times outright neglectful. I wasn't nourishing. That level of attention and care I showed for everyone else didn't apply to my body. There was little respect, integrity, patience, kindness, compassion, or curiosity in the relationship. I wasn't available or dialed in to the needs and cues my body was giving me—and, when it started sending bigger signals, I got frustrated with it for "acting up" and getting in the way of my life. If I had treated other relationships this way, or spoken to another as I spoke to and about my body … well, you can imagine that a thriving relationship would be short-lived.

Our personal relationship with our body is further challenged by the cultural messages with which we are bombarded. There are far more messages of shame, limitation, and complaints about our "wonder suits" than there are acknowledgments of its functionality, its miraculous ability to heal, or its power to enliven great vitality.

The potential and power imbued in our bodies is stunning. Yet, we aren't conditioned to see it, let alone harness it.

Within the vessel of your body lies the capacity to discover something you never knew of or believed was possible—to enliven something that has been buried, to reveal answers desperately sought, and to activate resiliency and growth. Your body is a major player in rising beyond your 911 with greater wisdom, strength, love, and grace.

"You've always had the power, dear. You just had to learn it for yourself." So goes the famous lines from Glinda the Good Witch in *The Wizard of Oz*. I've watched that movie hundreds of times, though for decades I did not internalize the wisdom bomb contained in that powerful statement. Not unlike Dorothy, we in Earth School walk a unique pathway that, when we are ready, can return us to the deeper truths that were within us all along.

THE EARTH VIEW OF BODY

If we've had this amazing potentiality all along, literally coded within us, how is it that so many of us are unaware of it, or do not know how to access it?

For my clients, part of the challenge is maintaining a healthy relationship with Body throughout the day. Many exercise regularly in the morning or evening. Yet, amid constant pressing demands, they push through long hours unaware of (or aware of, but not tending to) the cues their body offers. I was there, too. Working at a feverish pace to balance it all. I was everywhere at once, but also nowhere. I certainly was not grounded in my body, nor available to listen or respond in kind to its messages.

Positive body relationships are further strained by the constant influx of media feedback. We are told what an attractive body looks like, what kinds of clothes our body needs to wear, what kind of home our body needs to live in, and even how much sex our body needs to have.

We shove a lot of life down into our bodily container. We push our vessel hard, always promising rest in the future though rarely actually taking it in the present. We wrap it in an attractive bow while avoiding real connection with it. We try to control the signals it sends us, rather than actually listening to them.

We hold on so tight to the vision of what we want that we inadvertently strangle the beauty and life we have.

Layer on mainstream views that the body is limited—from early mechanist views that saw the body as a machine, to modern perspectives that suggest you are either blessed or doomed by your DNA—and you have a recipe for dissatisfaction with your earthly vessel.

If we perceive our bodies as perpetually flawed and in need of upgrading, it's no wonder we are disconnected from them. No wonder we put on blinders and ignore the signals our bodies send us. No wonder we live in our heads, locked into a perpetual state of problem-solving.

Yet, if you really listen to your body, you will *know* that your body is more than a fix-it project. It's exciting and empowering to realize that you have more power over your health than you may have been taught. You are not at the mercy of your DNA; lifestyle choices, emotional regulation, and stress management all play a role in genetic expression. Beyond that, there is an incredible intelligence and power within you, and it's been there all along. When you become willing to acknowledge and be with your body in a mutually-beneficial and respectful relationship, it will begin to reveal itself to you.

I'm sure you've noticed a theme throughout this book about our tendency to ignore, avert, avoid, and control as a means of navigating our experience in Earth School. We do this with our bodies, too—especially as we begin to feel the pressure of maintaining youthful appearances. *Fill in those smile lines. Use the latest and greatest anti-aging solutions. Beautify your hair color or use growth products to replenish loss.* The message is clear: "Don't let them see that you are aging."

Even those who do well with managing "healthy" routines often engage those routines in a disconnected, almost absent-minded way. Double tasking with a podcast or webinar while running or lifting weights. Inhaling food at your desk without tasting (or even chewing) it properly. Not fully noticing how your body responds to a new, healthy change in routine. If you're already doing all the "recommended" things, well done. The next level is actually *being present* with them and allowing your body to really absorb (mentally, physically, and emotionally) the gift of these health-enhancing lifestyle choices.

Nothing that is *You*—the true you—requires searching, striving, perfecting, or augmenting. The very act of searching, even under the guise of "being healthy," takes you away from direct access to the answers you seek and the expanded capacities and capabilities of Body.

So, what is the body actually meant to do? How is it meant to be employed?

As usual, Soul holds the answer.

THE SOUL VIEW OF BODY

You've come far enough with me to understand that you are more than you know yourself to be. And yet, have you included your body in that knowing?

As we've explored previously, you are a Soul who has a body. More specifically, you are a multi-dimensional energetic being who has a body to inhabit this dimension at this time. Body is a temporary assignment, a loan from the universe to support and animate your unique expression in the world. And yet, it is—as we explored earlier in this chapter—also your primary relationship, the only one that will be with you from start to finish in this lifetime.

In Soul View you are called to reappraise and release the limitations of politics, religion, and history that have devalued some groups based on gender identity, race, ethnicity, socio-economic status, or decisions we've made in the past. None of the above is *who you truly are*. All can influence your life, to be sure, yet they are not the whole truth of *you*. As you unbind your preconceptions, explore vast sources, and discern your truth, you will set yourself free in the bigger body of universal life.

No matter how you currently feel about your body, or what external influences conditioned your view of it up until now, I can promise you this: at some point *something* will direct you back "into" your body. Some event, situation, or feeling will shift your outward focus to the unfathomable, untapped ability within. The 911 can come in many ways, from the subtle to the overt, but it *will* come. And when it happens, you will have a choice: go back to treating your body in ways that are limiting or lean into exploring, and embracing, its true nature.

From a Soul View of Body, you have the capacity to unlock new layers of being, including optimized physical health, unleashed healing capacities, expanded intelligence and wisdom, and many other capabilities that lie dormant or under-realized. Only via the Soul View can we seize the expanded potentiality that lies within the material body. These gifts have been there all along, latent and unexpressed. As we've learned, the Earth View of Mind (which is steeped in the rational, logical, or proven) limits what we can enliven—yet that doesn't mean it's not available.

When you are willing to experiment with tapping into intelligence beyond what is known in physicality—as we have already begun to do—a universe without bounds becomes available within this bounded container of Body. Coupled with evolving understanding from science and medicine that reveals we are more empowered with DNA—by way of life-style choices, stress management, and the body's capacity for neurogenesis (cell growth) and neuroplasticity (cell adaption)—than previously understood, we begin to see that we can heal and thrive beyond even the most challenging conditions. Holy wow. And while it's true we don't *need* the confirmation of science to enable these capacities of Soul via Body, I do appreciate that for many (my former self included), knowing the science can make it *seem* more possible.

Rumi wrote, "Everything in this universe is within you. Ask all from yourself." When I first read those words, they ricocheted through me with a resounding, "Yes!" Although I wasn't sure precisely what the poet meant, I *knew* his words to be true. The expansive feeling, shivers coursing through my system, hair standing up on my arms ... it was *resonance.* My body was literally saying, *This is true. You know this to be true about me.*

Shortly thereafter, I also began to notice that, when I was about to make a decision that was not aligned with a deeper knowing, my tummy or shoulders contracted. Turns out, the body is a barometer of truth. It literally signals alignment to truth through expansion and contraction.

Decades ago, as an evidence-based psychotherapist, this would have seemed far-fetched or impossible to me. I've joked that I live a quick-turn karma life—meaning, that which I judge invariably comes right back to me in such a way that I am *invited* to re-explore and rediscover expanded understandings within it. (Well, at least once I get through the relearning or remembering part.)

Thankfully, life has a way of opening previously closed doors. And minds.

Feelings and sensations are just one of the body's languages. Vibration is another. Everything—even intangibles like ideas and emotions—vibrates at a different level. With higher frequency emotions, such as love, you vibrate at higher levels. Shame, jealousy, and anger vibrate at lower levels. Turns out, how you think, speak and feel, as well as your choices around food, music, books, furnishings, and stuff, all influence vibration.

You've likely already had experience with this, yet maybe you thought about it differently. You know that when you walk into a tranquil, clutter-free space you feel peaceful. You know that when someone shouts at you, you might feel tense and tight. You know when you "click" with someone, and have an instant rapport. You know when someone you love is lying. You know all of this because your body is translating the language of vibration on your behalf.

Communities have vibrations. Cities and towns have vibrations. Homes have vibrations. Airports have vibrations. Some, you resonate with; others, you don't. Either way, your body is communicating with the space, and the people in it.

The absolute beauty of Body is that, when you are aware of Body's capabilities and learn to listen to and speak with it, you can detect and shift vibration easily. Vibratory frequency is your ultimate creative agent; it literally creates reality and influences the flow of energy around you and through you. However, you can't think your way to a new vibration with Mind alone. Thoughts play a role; however, the most powerful key is the *felt* experience in Body.

This, my friend, is the ultimate paradox of life in a human form. While you *have* a body, you are not your body. Nor are you *of* your body. And, at the same time, Body—the vessel through which you are expressing in this dimensional reality—knows what Mind cannot.

As Dr. Sue Morter wrote in her book, *The Energy Codes*, "You are here as creative Source energy in a body."

Along the journey of my 911, I learned to work with Body through various kinds of energy work, healings, trainings, and movement practices. I started down these paths because they helped me calm my mind. What I didn't realize at the time was how much they would *matter.* And I mean "matter" literally, as energy presides over matter. As you enliven a greater field of imagination, and feel in the depth of your being *as if it was already true*, while day to day taking aligned actions directed by Soul and executed through Mind and Body, you will create a new reality. Consistency is key.

This requires more than a single ideation. Play. Let your imagination go *wayyy* big. Then, allow Soul to make it even bigger. Do this often. Watch how matter follows energy. This is all available to you through Body.

For high performers, a key aspect of the Soul View of Body is to learn how to be *in* the body, instead of just doing through the body all the time. Acts of connection, like the exercises I'll share later in this chapter, can feel "unproductive"—and when you are in search of the sacred, hearing the call of your Soul's 911, they are anything but.

Your body is a container of sacred truths. It holds truths from the past, across generations. It holds truths of the present. It resonates with the truths in music, words, and movement. Those shivers down your spine when you hear a certain song, the way your heart feels full when you hug your best friend—this is Body speaking its language of resonance.

With increased awareness and practice, your body becomes a bridge between heaven and Earth. It will speak to what vibrationally aligns with what *you* define as sacred—within you, around you, and beyond you. The key is learning to listen, to receive, and to *rest in yourself.*

THE BEAUTY OF THE "AND"

When it comes to Body, living in the "and" means living more fully, Soul to sole.

Having spent my entire adult life on overdrive, I was convinced I could never slow down and be "one of those meditating types." It would be impossible, I thought, for my busy brain to slow down enough to drop into my body—even if I wanted to, which I wasn't sure I did.

Turns out, it wasn't impossible. And once I stopped telling myself stories about the process, it wasn't even hard. It just took some practice, curiosity, and a bit of patience.

As a Soul living through Body, you can access and actuate the treasures of conscious awareness by facilitating the union of Mind, Body, Soul, and Heart. You can change, amplify, and generate new realities while using more and more of your potential in service to fulfilling life (your own and others').

Crucial to the *and* is being connected within Body to Soul, and being connected beyond them both to whatever you identify as your higher power(s). You may have heard comments about a person being a "lost soul" or "having no soul." I offer this: all with a body are a Soul. They are not "lost souls"; rather, they have lost connection with Soul via trauma. This disconnection allows them to act in ways that are not loving, and may even be dark or heinous. The human got lost or buried in layers of wounding. Our work is to find our way back to Soul (back *home* here in Earth School). Body is our pathway to this connection and reclaiming the eternal truth and presence we are.

It is important to know that your body, as part of the bigger body of life, can also feel the heaviness of the world at times. It may be confusing—especially when life is in a season of ease, yet you feel sad, angry, or weary. These are likely times when your body is responding to a larger body as a whole. Gratefully, the insights and practices offered here can be engaged for empowered benefit, whether the source of your unrest is internal or collective.

When you bring Body into the beauty of the "and," you can harness Body's intelligence and put it to work in your daily life. This will help you make more powerful decisions, follow your Soul's guidance, and live in a more aligned way. Energy is currency. As energetic beings there are so many easy ways through small actions to generate and transform your being and the greater collective body. Energy can never be exhausted; it can only change form. The good news is you get to influence the quality of energy you experience.

Working *with* Body

Most people try to access the union of Body and Soul through Mind, yet that's often the hardest place to start. It is easier (and more effective) to create space for the "and" by becoming grounded and centered in Body, as if you are rooting yourself deep in the earth. This will direct Mind energy into the body and meld it with Body's present reality. Then, with a simple touch on your heart space, you can direct Soul awareness into the center of your vessel.

Breath is the most natural and powerful way into Body. The act of consciously partnering with your breath has a very different impact within and on your body than automatic unconscious breathing. When you perceive a threat, real or imagined, your breathing changes. Coupled with grounding and centering, conscious breathing signals to the parasympathetic branch of the Autonomic Nervous System (ANS) that it is safe to relax. To the contrary, if there is a perceived threat, the sympathetic branch (the other branch of the ANS) signals a stress response (i.e., increased heart rate, shallow breathing, flight, or fight). The deliberate act of purposeful breathing (and other techniques such as humming and movement we've covered) serve to decrease or dismantle the stress response. From this place of safety and calm, you can attune to what is arising within your body and discern truth. Then, you can send the desired signals from Body to Mind to inform your next right action—an action rooted in Soul truth, wisdom, and love, rather than fear.

As you intentionally practice connecting with Body, reclaim your natural awareness, and deepen the relationship between you and your vessel, you will begin to decode the communication and feedback loop you used to ignore and override. You will begin, throughout your day, to attune to the signals through sensation—aches, pounding, throbbing, shooting pain, tingling, goosebumps, tightness, etc.—that speak to various levels of resonance, safety, truth, and integrity in your inner and outer world. As well, you will notice how you are receiving guidance in the form of "gut feelings," intuitive hits, and heart wisdom that empowers you to discern the next right action of support for the body.

The beauty of the "and," when it comes to Body, is about building a great relationship. And, like any great relationship, this will require an investment of time and attention from you.

Actively develop a loving partnership with your vessel, rather than staying in a space of "management" or command. Be willing to surprise yourself. Befriend your only lifelong companion in the way you do all of your other beloveds.

Another key strategy is to activate your physical senses more fully to elicit enhanced physical ability and higher-self solutions.

When you reignite your five senses, you raise your vibration by coming into *what is happening now*, rather than *what you have decided is happening now*. In the process of bringing your full awareness to what your senses perceive in this now moment, you release your certainties for a little while and allow new information to arise. The Expand Your Senses practice in the Mind chapter is a powerful practice for Body too.

I offer additional ways to practice vibrational attunement at the end of this chapter to experiment with. Sometimes you'll note an immediate positive shift in your vibration. Other times, it will be subtle, maybe even undetectable. I encourage you not to breeze by these or brush them off. There are many ways in which we disburse our creative energy—avoiding, distracting, burying, blaming, shaming, self-medicating, over-giving, over-functioning, and pushing too hard without rest. All inadvertently lower our vibration. So, too, can your environment, the stuff around you, and the people you hang out with. Accumulative practice around vibrational attunement will counteract these influences and help you determine where more aligned choices and boundaries are needed.

It may feel like the act of paying attention will lead you

straight back into your pain; and it may. However, no matter how you push your truths down or away, they will remain under the surface (and on the surface), playing out in various ways, until they are tended to. The art is in becoming aware of, and attending to, the emotional or physical pain while staying rooted in your core of truth in this current moment—versus the story of Mind, which can make it feel like the past is present and unsafe. We'll explore this further in the Gratitude chapter; for now, breathe. Allow these very small actions to relieve the drag and burden you feel in your body. Let Body be freed from the shackles of Mind and the physicality around you even for a few moments, and fill the space with breath.

It's important to take smalls breaks once per hour to close your eyes and breathe. Closing your eyes for 30-60 seconds gives the body a break from constant stimuli—the nonstop information, demands, and noise your body is taking in all day long. At the same time, you can reset and refresh through deliberate breathing. These very brief breaks build the habit of tending to your system regularly throughout the day, versus only during the morning or evening.

When you meet your body in the space of the now, try to embrace whatever arises. As I am sure you've experienced, "now" moments can vary greatly. The whiplashing stories of the Mind can move you from complete confidence to obliterated confidence; so, too, can the flow of feelings of Body. In one moment, you feel like, "I've got this." At another moment, you may feel shaken. Inadequate. Totally unable to sit still and concentrate. Too sensitive, or not sensitive enough. In all states, meet yourself with deep compassion. This is part of your 911, and the paradox of human life. Still, even amid very uncomfortable feelings, there is a place within where consistent peace abides.

Be mindful to not invalidate yourself because you are out of practice at communicating with Body. You have the same capacity to experience joy and wonder as anyone on this planet, and you have the same mechanisms for receiving wisdom from within. However, to receive, you have to be *present*, aware of Body and Mind, Heart and Soul, all at the same time. The more you practice, the more you will positively surprise yourself. Trust the interior wisdom of Heart and Soul to guide and harmonize Body and Mind.

You've got this. Truly.

We all get to begin again, many times, in this now moment. The truth of you is like the sun, which is always present. Temporary clouds may appear, however the sun is always there. In the same way, you can instantaneously choose to anchor in and return to the truth of who you are through Body, which is always present even when your attention is elsewhere.

Rest in yourself. Honor your vessel—with all of its thoughts, feelings, sensations, narratives, aches, pains, overwhelm, fears, and joys. Shower your nervous system with gentle breath. Ground in Nature and Her network of life forces. Allow yourself to *be* the unshakable calm you are as your truest nature. Summon it. Know it. For just a moment, inhale life force and feel *free*. Exhale worry.

There is no way out except through.

As your 911 is demonstrating, avoidance and denial will no longer work. As your life shifts, you are called to anchor within—to reconnect with Body to reclaim *embodiment*. This is the eloquent, elegant intelligence of Soul weaving the next becoming of you.

It is a *holy reassembling.*

Nature *and the* Body

Nature is a playground for your body, and one of your best allies in discovering your expansive capabilities via the vessel of Body. Through its diversity, it offers numerous ways to reconnect with your body in ways that speak to and enliven your Soul. It can ignite wonder and awe, peace and tranquility, connection and care. Most of all, it can remind you of who you truly are.

One reflection of Nature that blows me away is the fractal—a repeating pattern in nature that can mirror similar pattern formations in your body and in life around you.

Look at the stump of a tree, with its concentric rings. Then, look at your thumbprint. Both provide unique information true only for the individual tree and human. It's a shared sacred geometry.

If you lay on your back and gaze up at a tree with its branches and leaves, it looks a lot like your lungs on an x-ray. Both the system of tree branches and your human lungs impact functions related to breath and breathing.

Next time you cut open a red cabbage, or a head of broccoli, notice the crazy, beautiful fractals. All are a reflection, in some way, of you. All are a reflection of connectedness among all life force energy.

Bask in the sky. Get lost in the land. Nature is vital to your well-being; indeed, without her, we would not exist.

It doesn't matter if your current access to nature is the limitless terrain of mountains, forest, or ocean, or a tiny square of plants on a downtown balcony; you can still tap into the bounty of Nature daily. Engage your senses, pay attention, and see what Nature reveals to you. Drink it in. Literally bathe your cells with the scents, sounds, views, and expressions of love, support, and unlimited possibility all around you.

Uplifting your vibration is easy in nature. Allow her to help you embody your Body, and return you to the state of peace and love you are and desire to reclaim.

Practices

Sending Love

One of my favorite ways to work with vibration is to send loving thoughts—thoughts of peace, joy, and support—to someone who is tense or irritated, or when there is a block between you and them. You will elevate the state of your body by doing this exercise, and also change your vibration around your relationship to the person.

I recommended this exercise to one of my clients who was struggling mightily with a coworker. Every day for thirty days, she sent loving thoughts to this person, even as she still struggled with her anger. Several weeks later, she told me, "I don't know what happened, but we are actually partnering well. The tension is gone!"

My client was stunned. I was not. People respond to our energy and vibration all the time, whether we are aware of it or not. My client was sending love, even when at other times of the day she didn't feel it; the love vibration overrode the anger vibration in her body, and the relationship changed. Sometimes, we have to engage in the action before we feel aligned with the intention. This is a very simple practice (though challenging, at times, in execution, particularly when you are called to rise above your thoughts or feelings about another); yet, when applied, it creates tangible, powerful shifts.

Vibrational Attunement

There are countless ways to generate and embody higher vibrations of love, joy, peace, truth, harmony, and so forth. The results are truly life-changing.

Every day, choose one or two simple exercises from the list below. Be present. Really *feel* in your body the desired shift. If the ideas on the list don't resonate, feel free to create your own. Then, engage in three centering breaths, set your intention to raise your vibration, and begin.

- *"Firsts" of the day:* As you arise in the morning, consciously choose your first thoughts, the first words you say, the first food you ingest, and the first action you take, to be of high vibration. Select your *firsts* mindfully. Days tends to flow with more ease and joy when your firsts are of high-quality frequency. When life happens not-so-smoothly, this practice sets you up to respond and react from a position of love.

- *Attune your instrument:* Music, chants, movement, self-care actions or laughing all impact your body's vibration. You know how some music makes you feel alive and want to dance, while other songs make you feel at peace with a calming melody, and still others help you find that good, healing cry? Whatever energy and vibe you desire, choose accordingly. The array of choices is endless; get creative and enjoy. As a bonus, go lie on the ground. The earth vibrates, too, so let its natural electricity and resonance settle and raise your vibration.

- *Scan your home or office:* Take a look at the things in your environment. When something catches your eye, ask, "How does this make me feel?" If something is broken or tattered, or a space is cluttered, take action to remove it, fix it, or create more space. If an object gives you joy, drink in the memory again. Create the sanctuary of vibration you desire. Your body is responding all the time to all aspects of your environment, including all that touches or is put into your body. When you create high vibes within the body and in the spaces you breathe and live, goodness is sure to follow.

- *Receive:* For most of my clients, receiving is far more challenging than giving. Yet, vibrational harmony happens with the dynamic exchange of giving and receiving. The invitation in this exercise is to fully receive something each day. It may be allowing someone to hold a door for you, soaking up a genuine compliment, or allowing a helping hand on a project. Practice receiving support every day. The more you receive, the more you will want to give.

Tune Into Your Body

Find a quiet place and set an intention to be still. Give yourself at least ten minutes for this exercise.

- *Scan:* Close your eyes and scan your body. What do you notice? Is there any tightness, or are your muscles relaxed? Are you sore somewhere? What are you feeling and where is it showing up in your body? Are you hungry or tired? How is your energy?
- *Ask:* You can ask your body whatever you like. Here are a few options to experiment with. If you don't hear or sense a response, keep breathing and stay in curiosity.
  - What do you need right now?
  - Can you show me what needs attention?
  - Body, what do you want to tell me?
- *Attend:* Based on what you learned, what small action will you take to offer your body support and love?

Becoming Body-Aware

As you tune into the gifts of Body, you will start to thread a divine needle. You will begin to notice how different experiences cause a different response in your body—and learn to let your body guide your response.

And, when in doubt, ask, "Body, what do you need, and what are you telling me?" Let Mind and Body live in a divine communion in service to life, and in service to Soul.

It took me quite some time to befriend this miraculous vessel that is my body. The symptom messengers had to get a bit loud and uncomfortable before I really started to pay attention. Yet, when I did, I recognized what a marvelous partner I have in Body.

The shifts I made weren't huge, especially at first. Rather, they were a series of small awarenesses that created a cascade of positive results. I learned to be mindful of the vibrational impact of my environment, my food, and the people I spent time with. I rested in nature. I breathed. Often, these shifts didn't add more to my day; rather, I was simply more present while doing the things I was already doing, like eating or exercising. Today, my ulcerative colitis is completely resolved. Typically, my sleep is deep and restorative, and my muscles no longer carry unresolved tension. If erratic sleep or muscle tension does arise, I am quick to take restorative action. Lesson learned.

You, too, can change your relationship to Body. Our bodies are self-healing and self-organizing. They just need a little help from us. In a loving partnership with Body, you can begin to live into more of the unbounded, limitless nature of who you really are. Even if you have current health challenges, lovingly partner with what is available.

Our "wonder suits" all have different abilities, functionalities, shapes, and sizes. May we appreciate these containers through which we get to roam the Earth. May we appreciate what is, and also be showered with grace and love for what isn't. May our challenges serve us as well as our strengths, and may we do our best to care for and serve our bodies as the precious gifts they are.

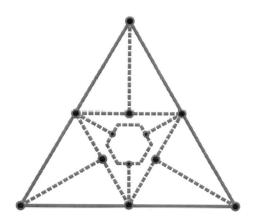

I am more than I thought myself to be.

The divine dances within, beyond, and all around me.

I am whole as is.

*I choose to live with expectancy of support and faith in
a benevolent universe.*

I never travel alone.

I am growing and thriving beyond this.

Joy. Love. Meaning. Contribution. Grace. Prosperity.

*All is possible when I live in and from the wisdom of
my heart.*

Chapter 7

Heart

I tune into my Heart to illuminate the way.

"Why isn't this working?"

In 2021, my client Rob was experiencing unrelenting stress at work. The continuing Covid-19 pandemic meant that, for a second successive year, his company wouldn't even come close to meeting its year-end targets. His employees were restless, stressed, and on edge; some had already quit, while others were threatening to leave if things didn't improve. The confluence of challenges was unlike any he'd encountered before.

Dealing with work stress was not new to Rob. He had decades of a demonstrated track record of successful results behind him and was known to be one of the best leaders in the company. But this time, it was different. None of the leadership skills nor strategies he knew were working. Previous incentives were no longer enough to satiate his talented and valued team. Two of his most senior team members had already resigned, and he feared more were soon to follow. Without the breadth and depth of talent he had purposefully nurtured over the years, the already-lackluster results were going to get worse.

It wasn't just work. His personal financial portfolio was tanking. His twin daughters, who had always thrived academically and socially, were struggling with depression. Between virtual schooling and limited contact with friends, their once fun and predictable life felt like it had been ripped out from under them.

As Rob and I were reviewing his numerous efforts at resolving these stressors, he shared how he kept hitting a dead end. No creative ideas emerged. No inspirational vision lit up the horizon.

Still, when I introduced the possibility of tapping into expanded solutions through connecting with Soul, he shut down. He had no belief in any sort of "higher power," he told me firmly. Intentions, prayers, meditation … they weren't for him. What he needed was just to keep diving in until his creative spark returned.

Weeks passed, and that spark didn't show itself. There was not even a glimmer, despite his rigorous efforts.

And so, Rob surrendered, and agreed to experiment with a simple meditation practice designed to help him move from Mind to Heart. He expressed concern that he "didn't have time for this stuff," and that he "might not hear any guidance anyway, because my analytical mind is so strong and reliable"—however, he was willing to try, and that willingness is all that is required for us to begin a new journey.

My client Barbara had a very different challenge to Rob. She had been working in the space of personal development for years. She believed in a loving universe and a higher power. She put stock in the idea that her heart held answers for her. However, she was confused by the messages she was receiving.

When we started working together, she had just ended her second relationship in three years. Both times, she had been sure the person was her lifelong partner, the soulmate she'd been seeking. Nevertheless, both times, the person turned out not to be "the one." Barbara was understandably confused. She thought she could trust her feelings—these seeming signals from her Heart and Soul. How could her heart have betrayed her so profoundly?

Though Rob and Barbara had very different belief systems, both were about to learn the wonders of Heart.

My 911 sent me in search of the sacred—and, as you know, this search was clothed in various experiences along my Earth School journey. Some I desired, others I most certainly did not. Yet, each was a vital thread woven through my life, and each, when followed, led me back to my heart.

Like Rob and Barbara, I reached a place where things were no longer working. The solutions of Mind were no longer sufficient. I was asked to suspend what I knew—to allow the old patterns to dissolve, and open to the unfamiliar.

It was agony, and ecstasy. It was my 911.

When some aspect of your familiar identity is stripped away and being the "old you" just isn't working anymore, you are being called to return to Soul.

Although we can be transformed through joy, most of us get complacent in smooth seasons of life; so we often grow most profoundly via struggle or loss. The challenges you face are blows that crack you open; only then can the light, which is already there, reach you.

What *is* Heart?

Long ago, when mystics and scholars spoke about "heart," what they referenced was not the physical heart. Rather, it was the Spiritual Heart—the conscious, mystical heart. Although we have supplanted that meaning in recent years with the medical definition, the truth of Heart remains.

The heart, like the brain, contains both physical and conscious dimensions. However, while we have different words for what lies between our ears (brain = organ, mind = consciousness), the heart is just ... the heart. Our language doesn't contain the nuanced, subtle layers of emotions and spiritual energies beyond the pump organ that powers our bodies.

Mind and Body are essential and invaluable on the path to answering your 911 and reclaiming the sacred in your life, yet their best roles are as supporting cast members. The restlessness, yearning, and fundamental holy reassembly so common to a 911 from your Soul invites you to explore and connect with the most powerful guide available—your Spiritual Heart.

It is my experience that you cannot feel complete or realize your fullest potential without establishing a connection to the profound energies and wisdom of Heart.

Here in America (and in the Western world in general), many of us think immediately of the physical in regard to Heart. We talk about "heart health," and fear that our hearts won't function properly. We try to eat right, manage stress, exercise—all to keep this physical heart happy. These choices feel prudent and are commonly understood to be in our wheelhouse of influence and impact.

As for the emotional space of the heart, many of us identify with it through the duality of love and fear. You undoubtedly recognize the power of new love—when you feel the swelling of potential and the desire to be your best self. At those times, like the Grinch expressed, your heart seems to grow three sizes inside you, empowering you to lead with love. Conversely, when love is complete or appears to be rejected, you feel the pain of a "broken" heart in your physical body, like shards of glass being driven into the center of your being.

And yet, this Heart of yours (and mine) is so much more than this. It is a magnet, a compass, and the scale on Which we weigh our Soul's truth. It is a conduit of divine light.

THE EARTH VIEW OF HEART

The common pathway through most any challenge is through the brain.

You're a learner. An achiever. You pursue ideals, advance

goals, and make plans you believe will lead to success (however you define it). You may even find yourself saying things like, "Use your head," or "This stuff isn't going to fix itself!"

Your brain doesn't like the in-between. In a space of unknowns, it feels incompetent, scared, and impatient. Unchecked, Mind spins up all kinds of wild iterations, often zooming in on the thousands of ways things can go wrong.

Yet have you noticed that Mind never tells the whole story? Rarely do the narratives of Mind remind you of how much you've grown, how resourceful you are, how you've thrived in innumerable ways or how even when you don't have all the answers, you still somehow always manage to make it through, usually even better than you thought amid the challenge.

Most of us long for the positive feelings associated with the emotional heart—like love, joy, happiness, and content-ment—but we try to "figure" our way to them through Mind. We fear not feeling good, so we employ Mind to guard us from hurt and betrayal. We assess risk when we could be exploring feeling. We cling to our identities even when they no longer fit us, because they correlate to what we want to be known and valued for. And when Heart does speak up, we shut it down or are reluctant to listen to what it has to say. If it isn't logical or linear, we've been trained to mistrust it.

A 911 is a call from Soul—and it is calling you back to your Heart. On the way, you will be asked to shed the false identities, securities, beliefs, and assumptions that keep you from fully entering your heart space. This is perhaps the most transformational part of the 911 journey.

Rob believed for most of his life that if he worked the plan, set goals, and did "the right things," that his success and happiness would be assured. Yet, when his 911 arrived, his safeguards failed, and his certainties were snatched away. In their place, he was asked to do something he had always dismissed: trust in something invisible that was nonetheless more powerful than himself, and allow for the light to illuminate what was ready to be revealed.

As you learned in the Mind chapter, we have more than one brain. In fact, we have three. In 1991, neuro-cardiologist Dr. J. Andrew Armour coined the term "heart brain." He discovered that the heart, like the brain, can process information through its over 40,000 sensory neurites (brain-like cells).

Since then, other scientists have uncovered more about the physiological connection between the heart and the brain. Studies have shown that, "There is evidence that the heart's brain possesses the capacity to learn, and even has short and long-term memory, and neural plasticity. Moreover, ascending neurological signals sent from the heart to the brain continuously interact with and modify the activity in the brain's higher cognitive and emotional centers."* This means that input from the heart can shape our thoughts, feelings, decisions, and identities.

According to research performed by the HeartMath Institute, the heart sends more information to the brain than the brain sends to the heart. Researchers wrote, "The heart is

---

* *McCraty, R. and Shaffer, F. "Heart Rate Variability: New Perspectives on Physiological Mechanisms, Assessment of Self-Regulatory Capacity, and Health Risk." Glob Adv Health Med, 2015 Jan;4(1):46-61. doi: 10.7453/gahmj.2014.073*

sixty times greater electrically, and up to 5,000 times stronger magnetically, than the brain. This awareness places the brain relatively weak in comparison to the heart."*

The Earth View with which we are familiar does not come close to encompassing the whole reality of Heart. And while the evolving scientific perspective on the heart's capacities in recent decades acknowledge this, it is a powerful reminder of what was known long ago and shared in all kinds of texts, poetry, etc., long before it was proven.

There is another, even more subtle layer to Heart these wisdom teachers knew of—and this energy is key to understanding our 911 and thriving in all seasons of life.

THE SOUL VIEW OF HEART

The Spiritual Heart is Soul's primary instrument.

Put another way … if Soul had a band, Heart would be the lead singer. (Mind would be lead guitar, naturally, and Body the drummer, keeping the rhythm.)

The energy of the Spiritual Heart is the richest, vastest, and most visionary in all of life. This attuned Heart can discern truth directly from Soul. It translates the Souls knowing of *expanded potentiality*: the limitless intelligence, wisdom, and knowing of latent capabilities and capacities you can develop beyond what you've been told is possible or available to you in how we typically use the mind. It understands the value of

---

*https://wearechange.org/heartmath-part-1

emotional Heart to feel both joy and pain, yet is capable of separating temporary emotions from the truth of itself. It knows what will make the physical heart thrive and empower it to support other organs, and collaborates with the gut and brain to give the body its most powerful voice.

Your Spiritual Heart knows that you do not need to push harder, effort more, or receive more logical input to shape your decisions. Rather, it reminds you that true wisdom comes from within, and that the harmony, purpose, and connection you yearn for are accessed first and foremost via the gateway of Heart.

When you are in the energy of Heart, biases and filters do not exist. Your 911 may have arisen as a challenging or painful situation in your life, and yet your heart knows that this is fertile ground for self-discovery. If you are willing to anchor in your inner sanctuary, rest, renew, and receive next right actions, you will naturally step into greater alignment with your true, higher self. You will know Soul's truth and live from that knowing.

If all this sounds too "mystical" for you, I understand. Even so, I would be willing to bet that while your Mind objects, your Body and Heart knows this to be true. And when you let go or soften your resistance and become willing to connect with this well of wisdom, love, and grace within you … it's delicious. It's beautiful. It's a remembrance of who you are—a reminder that you are whole, and that you always have been.

The Spiritual Heart is a master of nuance and clarity. It can pull the veil away from your confusion and show you how all the dots of your life connect. For you, or through you, everything has purpose.

Barbara, who you met earlier in this chapter, feared that she had been led astray by her heart. Mind's logic made her heart wrong, because she was (understandably) unhappy with the outcomes of these relationships into which she had poured so much trust and hope. When she tapped into her Spiritual Heart, she was filled with an expansive new awareness. She came to understand that, although she desperately wanted those relationships to be right, in more moments than not, her lovers had shown her through word and deed that they were not ready for the connection that she desired. However, in the moments where they *had* been connected, she had received growth and a feeling of love beyond her wildest dreams—and so had they. She had been a teacher for her partners, just as they had been for her. This awareness created a whole new level of possibility for her in future relationships.

And so, having learned to use the awareness and attunement practices outlined in Body along with the Spiritual Heart accessing techniques you'll learn later in this chapter, Barbara dove into Heart, and came out with wisdom and discernment, ready to claim what she truly desired and not sell out for less.

It wasn't that she couldn't trust her heart, or the truth it revealed. It was just that she was relying upon emotions and what she wanted to feel (and did occasionally feel) as her truth. Secondly, she had forgotten to *keep* tuning in periodically to discern: "What is the truth now?" While fairy tales condition us to expect everlasting love, rarely does the truth of one moment last a lifetime. After all, a relationship is a dynamic interplay of truth between two sovereign beings, and truths—like all things—change with time. Sometimes change facilitates growing together in ways that are aligned and mutually beneficial. Other times, despite all effort or due to choices beyond our control, the growth and value exchange becomes complete. As difficult as that can be initially, only through dissolution is there space for even greater love to be received.

By spending more time in her Spiritual Heart, Barbara was able to move beyond the emotional whirlwind, find peace with her experience, and lean into Heart once more.

Yet another wonder of the Heart is that it can hold two (or more) seemingly opposite emotions simultaneously. As a result of her expansion, Barbara held both joy and pain. Over time, she was able to navigate this paradox with more ease. She didn't feel as topsy-turvy when opposite emotions co-existed, and she learned to settle in the steadfastness of peace and love that always abides in the Spiritual Heart while discerning her path forward.

As you read this, you may feel scared, defeated, unprepared. Your 911 may have created a sense of urgency, as it did for Rob, that pressures you toward "doing" to influence the outcome. Yet bringing forth new life—whether through actual birth or through the vehicle of a 911—will always ask more of you than you are comfortable with or feel ready for. Like Rob, you too can learn how to reconnect with Heart to receive how to best move forward—and so much more.

So, cry. Speak the injustice and pain of your present moment into the light of your Heart. Let them be enveloped with the arms of unconditional love, and hear Soul whisper: *It will be okay. Life is for you, and through you. I am here.* As you rest in this sacred space, you can free the dissonance.

THE BEAUTY OF THE "AND"

When you nurture the whole physical, emotional, and Spiritual Heart, you galvanize the full potential of Heart as a conduit for Soul, love, and light.

Put more simply, this is all about deepening your inner life.

All practices in this book nurture the physical and emotional heart. In particular, the grounding and attunement practices in Body, the settling practices in Mind, and integrating stillness in Soul help to create optimal conditions for receiving Heart wisdom. Additionally, raising your awareness and investing your attention on the physical and emotional aspects of heart health will go a long way toward inviting greater awareness in your daily life.

Particularly when it comes to Heart, living the beauty of the "and" is all about harmony. In a wound-up body, it's hard to notice, let alone access and trust, the higher wisdom of Heart. A good place to begin is with the basics. Movement helps to strengthen the physical heart and release emotional energy. If you don't already have a regular exercise practice, even a walk around the block while stretching your arms to the sky can get energy flowing again.

Caring for the emotional heart is also essential. You know those times when you feel totally alive, on point, happy, laughing, and carefree? Create more of *that*! Be mindful of the balance of life-illuminating versus life-draining experiences in your daily routines. (Hint: most of us need to boost the "life-illuminating" parts, by a lot.) So go ahead and put the joyful stuff on your schedule. Make a date with joy—and keep it.

On the flip side, make time to tend to the pent-up emotions, fears, disappointments, hopes, and dreams that you've bottled up for days, years, or decades. In the next chapter you will be guided through a practice for freeing pent-up emotions. The beauty of the Spiritual Heart is it can discern truth around emotions—meaning, it can tell the difference between what feels good or right in the moment versus what is actually conducive to long-term health and well-being. Emotion, without oversight from this wiser, mystical heart, is not necessarily the best advice-giver or the best barometer for truth. The more you enliven your Spiritual Heart in your daily life, the more clarity you will have around the feelings you've been suppressing, holding on to, or amplifying—particularly around your 911.

Connecting with the Spiritual Heart looks different for everyone. There is no singular path. My clients test and try different pathways of connection. From "active" connections—like a freeing run that "shuts off" their active mind, to rhythmic lifting of weights as they lose themselves in their favorite song, to nature hikes that foster a joining with majestic expansiveness—to quieter pursuits—like meditation in a distraction-free room, gazing into a candle flame or at a piece of art, connecting with a higher power, prayer, or sitting in the lap of a spreading oak tree. For me, after first aligning with a higher power and praying, deliberate deep breathing in solitude, and communing with nature are the most potent ways in.

Anything that allows the mind to soften and still, and that creates an "empty" space for listening and asking, can connect you to the Spiritual Heart. Access is guaranteed; all you need to do is set the intention, breathe, and tune in. This helps you get out of your own way. Although our individual life paths are varied and always will be, I encourage you to add periods of stillness to the mix daily. Our noisy, extraordinary world is filled with information overload; the power of stillness allows you to experience what lies beyond the noise.

I encourage you to make this connection a way of life versus a sporadic event. Over time, you'll find that nothing matches the level of intelligence, support, and love already available to you through your Heart. With practice, you will build trust and confidence in the guidance you receive in these connected moments. Also, find the time of day that works best for you to establish a clear connection. If you are usually spent after a long and stressful day, evening might not be the best time to try to settle in and connect; instead, try first thing in the morning. Personally, I tune in for two longer periods, morning and evening, to bookend my day, and incorporate very short periods several times per day. It may sound like a lot; it is, and it's not. Mostly, it's a deliberate shift in *how* I invest energy throughout the day—in the infallible conscious Heart versus the roller-coaster Mind story I often allowed before. Even one or two minutes of deep breathing between client calls can bring me right back into communion with the wisdom of Heart.

One more note about living in the beauty of the "and":

accessing Heart doesn't mean you will stop using Mind and Body. Your brain is vital and crucial, and so is your body as the vehicle through which you experience and navigate Earth School. However, only one source knows the next right action on your Soul's path, and that is your Spiritual Heart.

Go to your Heart before all, and you will never be led astray.

Working *with* Heart

As you play with the practices in this chapter and begin to tune into your Spiritual Heart, you may wonder what, exactly, you are listening for. Maybe you're asking yourself, "What is this 'wisdom' and 'guidance' I'm supposed to be accessing, and how will it actually show up?"

This intelligence can seem very subtle, particularly if this work is new and unfamiliar. As you begin, direct your awareness both within and around you as you move through your days. Intend to notice what you notice. The more you do this, the more this becomes a conscious way of being. Soon you'll begin to hear, see, feel, and notice constant communication and support throughout your days and night.

Here are several different ways guidance may speak to you. Though this list is by no means exhaustive, it will help you get a feel for the ways in which you can be guided daily.

- Thoughts may pop into your mind "out of nowhere" after you ask your Heart a question. Often, you'll "just know" what this information means to you.

- You may hear a loving voice speaking to you in words, images, or feelings.

- You may feel expansion in your body—like a hot air balloon filling up—when something is a "yes" for you. In contrast, you may feel a contraction in your body—like a tightening in your belly or shoulders, or a "sinking" feeling in your gut, when something is not in your highest good.

- You may receive images, sounds, smells, or even tastes as you navigate daily life or in your dreams.

- You may see numbers that carry significance for you.

- You may see animals cross your path or appear close to you. Each animal has a unique meaning that is relevant for you at the time it appears.

- You may hear certain words or song lyrics that feel significant or carry meaning for you.

- You may overhear a conversation or story that offers a clear solution for you.

- You may get lost in the beauty of Nature, watching a sunrise or a thunderstorm—and then, when you're relaxed, the exact inspiration you've been waiting for appears in your mind.

- You may experience synchronicities like a perfect person arriving or calling just when you most need support, or a clear sign to inform a decision you are wrestling with.

- You may receive "divine downloads" of inspired ideas, insights or visons, and other aligned moments that signal you never travel alone—help is all around you.

Whatever you notice, pause, and ask, "What does this mean for me?" Then, listen.

The intelligence of the universe is infinitely clever when it comes to reaching you through the gateway of the Spiritual Heart. Expect to be surprised. What you ask for may arrive packaged differently than you anticipate.

On the "author" page of my website, I've shared a picture of my writing table in the forest. I had asked for a writing retreat in the woods, and expected to be guided out of state. Instead, I found a forest practically in my backyard I hadn't even known existed until a neighbor took me on an impromptu walk past a dead-end road. I'd walked past this trailhead hundreds of times but had never noticed it before. And that neighbor? We had never walked together before, and we haven't since.

The more you engage with your Spiritual Heart's treasure trove of wisdom, the more synchronicities will happen. Something that you had hoped for, dreamed of, or desired will show up—and you'll just know it's more than a coincidence.

Sometimes, your guidance may challenge you. Some necessary changes are difficult and come with a cost. Yet isn't that true of all choices? There is a cost to change, and a cost for staying the same. However, your guidance will always be designed for your highest good, and for the greater good. Its essence will always be love-based. The more you ask, listen, and act, the more guidance you will receive, and the easier it will be to act upon, even when it feels big and a little scary at first.

THE HEART AND THE LIGHT

One of the most profound learnings on my own journey into Spiritual Heart has been coming to know myself and others as light. I seriously used to "LOL" at the suggestion that we are "light beings." (As an aside, we often judge what we don't understand or are not yet open to consider.) And the more I explored my 911 and listened to the inner calling arising within me, the more I discovered that light is ubiquitous. It is present in all cultures, across all beliefs, as the core of our nature.

Light is what connects your Spiritual Heart to your Soul and all else that lies beyond our five senses. It is the unifier between your inner and outer landscapes, heaven and Earth, spirit and matter. It is illuminating and discerning. It is the way-shower. It is love.

Without the presence of light-as-love, we lose our way. When love is not woven into the fabric of outcomes, it shatters relationships—between people, communities, and nations. Without love present, we create from scarcity, disempowerment, and fear. And yet, when we tune in, we realize that this is not the true way, nor is it our truth.

When I first started experimenting with bringing light into my heart, I would simply sit, breathe, and ask the light to fill my entire being and surround me. Honestly, I had no idea what to expect—or even whether I should expect anything at all.

To my great surprise, something remarkable began to happen. My perception changed. I was more open, more creative. I was able to let go and trust in situations that would previously have caused me to *control, control, control* for dear life.

Simply imagining a light growing within your heart can feel calming and empowering, and help you connect to something greater than you. You will notice that you think more clearly and expansively. As a "light being"—literally—you will notice that others are different around you. They'll say things like, "I feel good when you're around," or, "You light up the room!"

Light is everywhere. We just don't always have the technology to see it. And, just as there is light even in the darkest places in the known universe (including, as science is proving, within black holes), there is always light in our inner darkness, so long as we are willing to be in the dark and simultaneously settle into the knowing that light is always present. When we embrace darkness, we learn that we can "see" in the dark with the eyes of Soul and through Heart illumination. It is the light of all that we are as multi-dimensional Souls.

This light is what is missing from our understanding of Heart.

Of course, darkness is also essential to creation. Most of us fear it—particularly the "spiritual darkness" that is often inherent to a 911. Yet, whether the dark is like the dark of the soil in which beautiful things will grow, or of the womb, or of the sky at night, there is life blooming and being nurtured, even when the light seems as far away as the stars.

So, test and try. What would it be like to be, as Elaine MacInnes coined, "light sitting in light"? What would it feel like to summon light into your heart, rather than waiting for it to find you in the dark?

Nature *and the* Heart

Something magical happens when you are out in Nature. Our lives and troubles feel smaller when we are on the land. We get grounded and realize that we are part of something bigger. The air is fresher, the colors more vibrant. Our once-thrashing thoughts and the flash floods of cortisol in our bodies slow or cease. If we allow it, the gentle winds can carry away our worries, the earth will absorb our fear, and the mountains remind us to hold steady.

If you're not used to being in nature as a practice, all of this might sound like hippie poetry to you. This is your invitation to give it a whirl. Go explore. Be present in nature and see what experiences arise. There is a feast of beauty and goodness awaiting you on many levels. There is plenty of research to demonstrate that time spent in nature has a calming effect on people's minds and bodies, can lower blood pressure, and reduces stress hormones. Hooray to optimizing health and feeling more fully alive and renewed.

Still, well beyond physical benefit, a whole new world—or, more accurately, worlds—awaits you. You don't need to do anything special; you need only be present and dial in as awareness. Then, allow your heart to open—you can literally visualize doors opening in your chest if it helps—and feel the natural world. What is the Earth, or the wonder that catches your eye, whispering through your heart?

I treasure the times when I immerse myself into land and sky—when I can lay back in wonder at the majesty of trees, ground my bare feet on stone and dirt, and empty my vessel of stress and worry. In this stillness, I more easily attune to Heart, and come to know things I previously did not. Wisdom flows through with ease.

Nature is one of the easiest playgrounds on which to begin opening to the vast capabilities of Heart. You will feel the settling and expansiveness within. You will see, hear, and learn from the creatures, and from the rhythms of the land around you. When you connect with the infinite sky and its many reflections, you won't be able to contain your wonder about the great mystery of life and of life beyond and around you.

Practices

If you are new on the path to exploring your Spiritual Heart, start by simply dipping in. Honor that this is an unfamiliar practice and may feel a bit "out there" or uncomfortable for you. Like any good relationship, it's helpful to start slow; it will take time, attention, and nurturing for you to gain trust.

If you are already on a path of heart-centered practice, these exercises will still benefit you. Approach them with "beginner's mind" and see what arises. Your Heart may have some beautiful surprises in store!

Prepare

- Ask yourself: "Where in my life am I open to guidance?" Make a list of what you would like guidance on. It can be anything: relationships, money, career, health, or a particular next step or decision you are struggling with. If you are unsure, it's all good. What needs to arise will arise.

- Ask yourself: "How willing am I to be guided?" Take a spin through the list you just made. In what areas are you actually open to receiving guidance from your Heart? If you are skeptical, it's helpful to start with a small yes-or-no decision (like an invitation to an event, or a non-emergency determination on a work issue); this decision should be one that you consider important, yet one you are also open to experimenting with.

Ground, Drop In, Ask, and Listen

- Go and sit in a quiet place (outside in nature if possible). Close your eyes. Tap the ground.

- Set an intention to be open and clear. (*I am empty of preconceived ideas.*) Breathe to your own rhythm. After several breaths, put your hand on your heart.

- Imagine that there is a "wisdom chamber" in your heart with a door you can open. Breathe. Then, open that door. (If you have difficulty visualizing, you can speak the words: "I see the wisdom chamber." Breathe. Then continue, "I am opening the door.")

- Ask a question about the area you selected in your preparation exercise, either aloud or to your heart.

- Listen for the answers. If you find your mind wandering, come back to your breath. Touch the ground. Touch your heart. Settle in.

- You may end the practice when you feel ready. Whether or not you "heard" guidance, it's all okay. Sometimes its instant in the practice, other times it reveals itself in various clever ways later.

Sit In the Light

This is a meditation intended for those who are already comfortable with accessing the Spiritual Heart. However, feel free to try it regardless of your experience level—your heart will know what to reveal.

- Find a comfortable seat, or lay down in a Śavāsana-like posture on your yoga mat.

- Close your eyes. Breathe deeply. Touch your heart, or just rest your attention there.

- Imagine the life force of our central sun, with golden-white rays streaming ever-so-gently down from the sky. Imagine those light rays entering the top of your head, and moving slowly down your body. Along the way, see the light entering every organ, cell, node, tissue, bone, artery, and vein in your body.

- When your body is full, imagine the light streaming beyond you, out through your feet and into the rich layers of the earth. Let Earth herself receive this light. Then, feel Earth gently return this light to you, sending it up through your feet and your entire body.

- Imagine that the light you have absorbed is collecting in your heart and merging with your Soul's light. You are now radiating light from your heart in all directions—in front of you, behind you, above you, and below you.

- Rest in your breath and the stillness of the light. If you are so moved, touch your heart with your fingertips.

- Now, ask whatever you'd like. Or, just say, "I am listening. Show me the way."

- As you receive downloads, whispers, or glimpses of possibility, ask any questions you have. Engage the light as a source of intelligence.

- When you feel complete, simply say, "Thank you." No matter what happened (or didn't happen), the connection with light alone is powerful and signals your readiness to receive.

- Take a few final breaths. Open your eyes and wiggle your fingers and toes. Then, go on with your day or evening.

Becoming Heart-Aware

The more you work with Heart, the more you will come to understand that resting in Heart is all about surrender. Not solving, fixing, begging, controlling, or directing—just being. Breathing. Listening. Joining with ease, relinquishing all preconceptions.

Sometimes, in surrender, you will receive a sign in one of the ways we explored earlier. Or maybe, you will come to understand that you may never understand the whole of what is unfolding for you and through you—and rather than railing against that, you open to the possibility of acceptance, and ask to cultivate or be filled with the courage, grace, and strength to move forward. Accepting what is may not relieve us of all stress and suffering, yet it lessens with time and as you return again and again to the Spiritual Heart. Here, your deepest knowing, wisdom, and unshakable love will renew you and assist you to spread your wings to once again soar. For this Heart knows exactly how to support you.

We are part of something bigger than any one of us. Ultimately the Spiritual Heart guides us to realize that we each have a higher destiny, and that within us is the potential to enliven it for the good of all. "Higher destiny" does not have to mean grand achievements, although it might. Being a blessing to one person is incredibly powerful and creates energetic ripples that touch lives in ways you will never know.

So, surrender. Breathe. Drop into the energy of Heart and listen for what it says. Attune to your surroundings, where messages also abound. Not only will you receive the answers you are seeking around your 911, you will also, with time and openness, gain the keys to unlocking your true potential in service to life.

For Rob, accessing the Spiritual Heart felt like a stretch. It ran counter to his belief that there was no higher power (within or beyond), and that Heart was just a muscle. Still, he was willing to give it a spin. He started by asking for guidance in little ways, like dinner ideas (yes, the invisible is always speaking, even in our most basic daily decisions). He later progressed to sitting for guidance with his girls, and for what felt like the untenable work context. To his great surprise—even though he could not logically make sense of it—he began to receive and generate creative visions and guidance. When acted upon, this guidance resulted in him challenging company policies around remote work. As a result, the resignation trend ceased, and his team is more engaged than ever. Months later, he followed up on "a hit" (as he came to refer to guidance) to explore an atypical partnership that has since become instrumental to the company's rebound and growth.

Along the way, he also learned to settle into the unknowing with regard to the business and his financial portfolio. He started to make connections about events in his life that he'd never seen before. This enabled him to relinquish his stronghold of control and lean into trust that something else was in play. He's still not sure how he would describe it, yet he is now convinced there's something bigger going on in his life. He now looks forward to the daily connection with Heart; it feels like the wisest friend and mentor he's ever met.

And, beautifully, Rob introduced simple practices of Heart with his daughters. They have bounced back from their depression and are now lively, thriving teenagers again, even amidst the continuing challenges of the pandemic on school life.

Barbara is nothing less than blown away with how she understands and walks through life now. Learning about the nuanced heart—and in particular learning to commune in the Spiritual Heart—has been life-changing and freeing. She owns her truth, and her relationships (romantic and otherwise) are now of the quality, reciprocity, and joy she had been searching for. She sees the miraculous around her, and expects to be supported.

I am astounded by the all-encompassing nature of Heart. Whether it is the physical heart that makes life possible, the emotional heart that provides the range of felt experience that makes life exquisite, or the transcendent Spiritual Heart wherein you can remember all you are and came here to be … Heart is profound.

In the energy of the mystical heart you can rest and renew in your true nature. When life feels upside down, this ever-steady love and peace are just what we need to help us through. At the same time, you will connect to the illuminator of your inner oracle and its gifts of expanded potentiality. Only with this can you reveal your highest expression, and live in true connectedness with all, both visible and invisible.

If you find yourself still unsure whether this cosmic heart is for you, draw from the strength of my belief in you, and in the power of your Spiritual Heart, until you cultivate your own. I know something incredible is waiting for you.

I tune into the precious moments of each day.

I am excited to receive the love notes available within each experience.

Gratitude reverberates through my cells and radiates to all.

Chapter 8

I generate Gratitude for all that was, is, and will be.

"This wasn't how it was supposed to go ..."

For months, my client Amanda had been focused on what was displeasing and challenging about her role within a well-known investment management firm. She could do her job in her sleep, and while she excelled at delivering extraordinary results and leading a highly engaged team, the "juice" was gone for her.

She told herself she "should" feel grateful for her incredible career, this amazing role, her huge salary, benefits, and her devoted team—nevertheless, those feelings just kept slipping away.

Then, one day, a surprise meeting with her boss turned her world upside down. The division Amanda led was being divested and acquired by another firm. Her role was deemed redundant. By the end of the year, her employment would be ending.

"Nothing personal," her boss said. "It's just business."

Amanda could not believe what was happening. Yes, she'd been discontent, but she'd never let it show … had she? Her thoughts were an incessant drumming. "You are no longer needed. You are no longer wanted." Of course, that wasn't what she had been told, yet after so many years of dedicated service, sleepless nights, and insane deadlines, she couldn't help but feel left out in the cold.

All that she had taken for granted—the mission, the clients, her team—she now deeply missed.

"What should I have done differently?" she asked herself. "This wasn't how it was supposed to go! Was I 'too much'? Did I advocate too much for my team? Should I have just fallen in line?"

And, the biggest question of all: "Who am I now?"

For the first several weeks after she was let go, her mind was a hellish companion. Her busy brain was ruthless in its criticism and comparison. Her sleep was erratic and unsettled. Her appetite was insatiable, and she was regaining weight that she had worked hard to lose.

Did Amanda feel lost? Yes. Betrayed? Certainly.

Grateful? Not a bit.

Little did she know that this unfolding of events was life speaking to her—a 911 from her Soul to call her in the direction of long-buried dreams.

Amanda had always wanted to travel the world and build

homes for underserved populations—people who didn't have the means to make a comfortable home a reality. This was personal for her. As a young child growing up with a struggling single mom, she remembers bouncing like a ping-pong ball from one temporary living situation to another. Her mom was loving, bright, and hard working—she held multiple jobs and went to night school—and was doing the very best she could. Although Amanda had other adults she could turn to in her mom's absence, she often felt alone. It was also tough for her to make friends, and when she did, she feared her joy would be stolen away by the inevitable next move.

By the time she was a teenager, Amanda's life came into more harmony and ease. She and her mom finally had their own home, where they lived through Amanda's high school years. The relief of this stability was indescribable—yet, it took her a while to trust this new steadiness.

Post-college, Amanda was on fire, determined to create a life of abundance and predictability—one that would afford her the home, the stability, and the freedoms she had dreamed about as a child.

A decade before her layoff, she'd led her team in a week-long joint venture with a construction company that built homes for low-income families. She recalled to me the celebration where the keys to the home Amanda and her team had worked on were turned over to the family. "That look in their eyes," she recalled. "Those tears of gratitude. The kids jumping up and down. I'll never forget it. I laid in bed that night and thought, *Someday, I'll do more to make a difference for people who don't have stable homes*. But I never did anything like that again."

Now, life had shifted in the blink of an eye. She had the time, and she had the money. What would she do?

After reconnecting with Soul, Amanda made the bold move to pursue a new role—one that was aligned with the dream in her Heart. She decided to invest her talent and passion in a position with a global organization whose mission was to create housing for low-income families and individuals.

Compared to her previous role, the title, money, and prestige seemed like a huge step down. However, her inner fire—joy, alignment with Heart and Soul—was burning at an all-time high.

Did she still feel lost? Not one bit. Betrayed? Not a chance. Grateful? Beyond words.

Soul and Heart always know the way. It just takes Mind a little while to catch up sometimes.

What *is* Gratitude?

As I traverse the trails, the view is mesmerizing. The captivating beauty simultaneously takes my breath away and gives me breath. The air is crisp yet gentle. As I pause under the awning of trees, the nearby pond is a mirror image of the rich hues of autumn: warm golds, vibrant pops of orange, ruby reds, and vivid greens. The squirrels are playing tag; I giggle.

All the while, I breathe in fully, drinking in this goodness. I am immersed in this moment. Utterly alive.

It's true what they say: deeply felt gratitude enlivens joy, peace, and inner harmony.

Gratitude is delicious. In your most grateful moments, your whole being feels uplifted. You think higher-quality thoughts. Your body feels full of light as your Spiritual Heart expands. This "enlightenment" ripples back to you as you emanate more joy and excitement.

Gratitude is a simple act, yet so profound. You may never even know how sharing gratitude rekindles the light of a fatigued fellow Earth-dweller. It can be the act that changes the course of someone's day or even life. Conversely, if you are in a funk and receive unexpected support or appreciation, boom! A boost of momentum is stoked. It's like you've just remembered that you matter, that you belong here, that you are loved.

More than anything, gratitude is an amplifier. When applied mindfully, it enables you to connect with the awe and wonder of your life in all of its ordinary expressions. This appreciation magnifies the light within you, and makes it possible to see a more expansive view of life, love, and purpose.

Gratitude is nosh and nectar for your Soul.

However, let's be honest: living fully dialed in to the awe and trust that real gratitude requires can feel nearly impossible—especially during a 911. When you've lost something or someone, or received life-altering news, its normal to experience a whole range of emotions like shock, denial, anger, anxiety, sadness, betrayal, hopelessness, and overwhelm. You start running through all the ways in which things like this shouldn't happen to good people, nice people, young people, or people who plan well and do the right things. Thoughts like

I'm going to lose it! tumble through your head as your brain cycles through dread-and-doom scenarios and your intense feelings bow you down like a crushing weight. And if *you* were the one whose choices caused hurt, or triggered the outcomes that precipitated the 911, the rational mind can be even more relentlessly cruel.

It's during these times that gratitude's superpowers make themselves known. Like tender arms cradling you amid grief and the daunting and disconcerting unknown, it soothes you, settles you, and shows you how to navigate the next steps.

There is sacredness in endings. In order for something new to emerge, something old must be released or transfigured. This doesn't always happen in a literal sense—although it can—rather in a sense of dismantling paradigms, certainties, and identities that have run their course and are now complete.

Gratitude is one of the best ways I know of to dance with the paradox of both the light and the dark of life. We know growth takes place through adversity—and although that can be hard to remember (or appreciate) when you're buried in the fertile ashes of an old life, it is always true. The anchors of gratitude—beauty, thankfulness, awe, grace, and love—illuminate and expand your view when you enter the void of rebirth, reminding you of support both visible and invisible.

THE EARTH VIEW OF GRATITUDE

An Earth View of gratitude often includes expressing thankfulness or appreciation for something, someone, or some experience. If you've experimented with some of the gratitude practices taught by popular self-help influencers, the concept might conjure visions of journaling, meditation, or dropping notes in jars. This kind of mindfulness, which requires you to pause and reflect, is beautiful, and I highly encourage it.

There are many heartwarming stories of wonderful, generous people who extend acts of kindness to coworkers, family, friends, and strangers in need. Those stories remind us how much giving to others contributes to the greater well-being of the whole. It's the best of humanity, shining brightly, reflecting care and concern; it's inspirational and aspirational, reminding us that we can create the kind of world we all hope for and crave.

Science confirms that gratitude undeniably changes your life for the good. Feeling grateful affects your brain and biology as "feel-good hormones" of dopamine, oxytocin, serotonin, and endorphins are stimulated and released, uplifting your thoughts, feelings, mood, actions, and health. This, in turn, informs the way you see and experience yourself, others, and the world.*

Gratitude also increases your ability to self-regulate, and boosts your immune system. With elevated thoughts and emotions at play, you can reduce mental, emotional, and even physical pain. The broad positive impact on your body is remarkable. As a result, your overall well-being improves, creating even more positive experiences in relationships, work, and play.

The idea of gratitude from this Earth View seems easy

---

https://www.health.harvard.edu/mind-and-mood/feel-good-hormones-how-they-affect-your-mind-mood-and-body and appealing. However, the reality is that, in this fast-paced, multi-tasking, never-go-anywhere-without-your-device world, gratefulness is also easy to forget. Especially when life feels like smooth sailing, it's tempting to dismiss your vast reservoir of daily gifts—like the body that supports you to live and move in all the ways you do, the comforts around you that make daily life more fun and easeful, and how the people and resources of life around you support and care for you. When was the last time you were grateful for running water, the trees outside your door, or the hands that make it possible for you to do your job? Chances are, the busyness of life pushes these privileges right out of your mind. I, too, have lost sight of these huge blessings; what is commonplace often goes unnoticed until it is altered or taken away.

There's another layer here, too. If we are honest, the Earth View of gratitude is often conditional. When experiences line up the way you want them to, when people behave like you think they should, or when a project goes like it was supposed to, it's easier to feel grateful. It can feel a lot harder to cultivate feelings of gratitude when you feel taken advantage of or betrayed, when something undesired unfolds, or that project you've spent months working on goes off the rails.

Some of the most poignant lessons I've learned about gratitude have been from the hospice clients I've worked with. As I shared earlier in our journey together, they have been some of my most inspirational teachers. Even in periods of excruciating pain and fear, they found something to be grateful for. There is truly no time or situation in life where gratitude is misplaced.

THE SOUL VIEW OF GRATITUDE

The Soul View of gratitude is even vaster and more life changing than the Earth View. It expands what you see, how you see it, and what you value. It changes the way you create meaning around your life and life experiences—and when it comes to aligned living, meaning is undeniably powerful.

Early in my psychotherapy career, I partnered with clients who had experienced significant traumas. I marveled at their ability to process their history and create meaning that empowered them. Despite everything they'd been through, they were determined to ensure that their painful pasts served a purpose, and that the past did not consume or hold hostage their future. Their traumas became fuel for personal missions, goals, dreams, and service pathways.

Most of us have never lived the kinds of unfathomable life experiences that these clients did. Yet, all of us have struggled in some way to create generative meaning around life events and situations. Whether you got cut off in traffic, were passed over for a role, or were hurt by a significant person in your life, you told yourself a story about what the event meant and what it said about you. With Soul leading, you can lean into gratitude to cultivate a meaning that is respectful of self and propels your desired way of being. Instead of "How dare you?" you might think, "Thank you, other driver, for reminding me to slow down." Instead of "I'm not enough for them" you might think, "This role must not be the perfect one for me, otherwise Soul would have guided me there. What else is on the horizon?"

In addition to generating different, more empowering meanings from everyday events, when living from a Soul View, you invite greater presence. In fact, Soul challenges you to be fully alive and present for as many of the 86,400 seconds in each day as possible. This is more than a once-daily practice; it's a way of living and moving in the world. When gratefulness becomes engrained in the fabric of your life—when it's your filter, your sight, and the baseline from which you interpret and move—you become an embodiment of grace.

Between the bookends of waking and sleeping, you notice how the universe sends you daily love notes in the cleverest of ways. You receive constant confirmation that you are guided, protected, and loved. With intention and attention, you develop the skill of noticing these messages everywhere.

Once, I asked my Spiritual Heart and Soul for guidance about how to handle a delicate situation with a particular person with whom I was challenged. Moments later, I noticed that one of the leaves on the basil plant I was watering had a very clear heart-shaped hole in it.

I paused, breathed into my heart, and listened.

My heart spoke. *Find love—it's always here. Listen beneath the words and see beyond the actions.* I immediately attuned to gratitude. There was a lesson for me in this challenge. I offered thanks to Soul for helping me see it.

When I next saw the person in question, I listened beneath their words, and looked beyond their actions. What I saw was someone who felt underappreciated, unseen, and unworthy. They were hurting.

I was able to find examples and genuinely express my gratitude to them for how they had positively contributed to our shared experience. From that point on, our interactions changed for the better. They knew that they mattered and were valued. What a difference that makes. I was different too: thanks to Soul and a basil leaf, I was more deliberate from that point on in leading with open, love-based energy and modeling who I want to be as I engage with others.

Through the Soul View of gratitude, you can more easily notice and dial into what *is* working in your life, and spend less energy on what isn't. It helps to loosen the grip of criticism and "not-enoughness," soften your gaze, and expand your thinking beyond judgment and into grace. This creates an opening for you to see, hear, and explore a canvas in life that extends beyond you and your personal perceptions and goals. When this happens, magic unfolds. The Soul View ignites a sense of wonder and curiosity about the mystery and magnificence of life.

Questions about purpose, the greater intelligence in play, and the connectedness of all life start to bubble up. Though others across the region or globe once seemed distant, there's a growing seed of care and recognition that what happens to one, happens to all. You may even find yourself galvanized to make a difference with a broader cause with animals, the oceans, underserved people, climate change, or some other cause near and dear to you. This may be something you've cared about for a long time, or something that you hadn't given much thought to before (or even held opposing beliefs about). Either way, it will be a revelation and a call to act.

The core of embodied Gratitude is a billion shades of love. From the Soul View of Gratitude, you set the intention to *be* love, to lead from love, and to see love everywhere in the fabric of your life. More, you choose to feel love regardless of the circumstances you are dancing in right now and embody a broader trust in life and your own divine nature. It's rather remarkable how it all just flows together.

When you make gratitude a cornerstone of your way of being, you will not only find opportunities to be more grateful in the here and now, you will also remember the many times when you were offered grace from others in messy moments. Maybe you were miraculously extended a much-needed break, or a door was opened for you in a way you couldn't have accomplished on your own. Maybe a higher power intervened for you when you just couldn't get out of your own way. With gratitude, you can trust and have faith even if it previously felt impossible to do so.

You have it within you to discover and create a generative meaning of pain and struggle. Gratitude is like a guardian and mentor that can assist you in navigating darkness. It rearranges your perception from resentment, hate, jealously, and hopelessness to possibility, and the feeling that, with time, there just may be a way through. Gratitude helps you rekindle the light within that feels dimmed (or even absent) and guides you back to the remembrance that light is never truly extinguished. Light is always within and beyond, even when it cannot be felt or seen around you.

Most of all, gratitude reminds you that you have the power

to cultivate and choose meaning on the other side of your 911 experience, even if how to do that is not clear to you right now.

The more that Gratitude becomes your way of being, the more resilient you become. With heightened awareness, you can meet *all* of life with more appreciation, satisfaction, hope, and joy. The times of joy become even more vibrant. And in seasons of challenge, you more easily embrace paradox as you surrender into darkness. You come to know there will be times of great delight and times of great pain—and that, in Soul View, you can have a deep and loving relationship with both. Anchored in your true nature, with your higher power and helpers you may not be aware of on your side, you *know* there is *always* a way back to the place where the light dances and your Heart soars free.

Along the way, you set yourself up to continually receive more goodness. All the micro-moments you have cherished with thankfulness act as a magnetic attraction force for the bounty of life—because even life appreciates being appreciated.

THE BEAUTY OF THE "AND"

The "and" around gratitude is to incorporate both the Earth View and Soul View into your daily life.

Yet, how do you *live* from gratitude?

The art lies in consciously living from your Spiritual Heart. This empowers you to dial into the many moments of your daily experience with wisdom, love, and gratefulness. Your Soul forms the lens of your understanding as you pause and choose the quality of your next action.

To make this come alive, let's start with the contrast of unconscious automatic habits.

Most likely, you already brush your teeth twice a day and say "thank you" when someone offers you a kindness. You do these things so naturally that you don't consciously deconstruct the activity before you do it—you just do it. At some point, you connected with a reason why this behavior mattered (i.e., cavities or courtesy) and developed a route and reminders to trigger yourself to do it.

This automatic action taking can be wonderful. And, when you add gratitude to the mix, there is greater opportunity to consciously develop and stay aware of how and why you are moving through the world.

Most of us need a bit of help to slow down and notice all that we have to be grateful for, and to stop blowing by the thousands of moments that show us how life is speaking to us and supporting us. It can be helpful to start small by simply recommitting to living with gratitude. There are innumerable ways to do this; here are a few ideas to spark your creativity.

- Put a Post-It note next to your bed to remind yourself that the first words you speak tomorrow will be words of appreciation.
- Put a note in your calendar to call two people you value each week. Tell them why they matter to you, or share something you appreciate or value about them.
- Start a gratitude journal. Each night, write down three things: one experience where you were

supported (by a person, your body, or life), one experience or thing you were grateful for over the course of the day, and one experience or thing you feel satisfied with. (The last is important: high performers often forget to feel satisfied each day, as the focus tends to be on what is not yet complete.) Feel the lightness and joy of gratitude infuse your body as you recall and enliven appreciation.

• Set an alert on your phone that reads "grateful," and let life surprise you.

Simple enough, right? It is, and it isn't. To engage in the activity you choose with intention and full presence will require from you a different level of attention and awareness. This is not another action item on your to-do list; rather, it's a conscious reconnection with the feeling of gratitude and joy in your body, mind, and heart.

Another way to develop walking through life with gratefulness is to relive treasured memories in vivid detail. Experience them again as if they were happening right now. What were you wearing? Who were you with? What was the landscape? What were the colors, the sounds? What makes this memory so special? Let your cells bathe in the joy, appreciation, or care—whether for a micro-moment or an hours-long shower of love. This is really powerful when done right before an important meeting or engagement; note afterward how the exercise affected the quality of the interaction or experience.

Finally, notice how life is meeting you in the moments of your day. Whether you are on a walk, in a meeting, or hanging out with your family, deliberately direct your awareness to what is unfolding right in front of you. If your mind is tempted to wander, bring it back. Ask yourself, "What, in this moment, am I noticing?" Then, pause, listen, and give a nod to life for whatever was offered to you.

If you are going through a 911 right now, simple practices like these are invaluable in both honoring the struggle and kindling a knowing that spring always follows on the heels of winter. In *A Course in Miracles*, there is a statement and practice: *"I am willing to see this differently."* When you open to gratitude as a way of life, you plant a seed of readiness and possibility to see things not as you preview them, but as they truly are.

This *willingness to see differently* is a game changer. It can dissolve deeply held narratives and expand the playing field of perception. For example: I was not grateful at the time for my divorce. Yet, in time, anchored in the wisdom of my Soul, I was able to genuinely feel gratitude for the love and joy that once was, and for all that grew out of the relationship, including our two beautiful children. The best news is, two decades later, we are still friends and co-parent really well together, aligned in a shared mission of the highest good for our kids.

Gratitude is the golden, silken thread weaving together the collage of your life experiences. You may never understand the "why" of various experiences from your human vantage point, especially those involving great sadness. And yet, as you encapsulate gratitude, you will come to know you are part of the grander fabric of life, and that, through the whole of your experience, lives were indelibly changed for the better.

Perhaps one of those lives was yours, and perhaps those lives belong to people you will never know. Yet, in this intricately interconnected web of life, someone grew, someone loved more, someone is wiser, someone is kinder, because of you.

Working *with* Gratitude

So far, we've gone through a lot of "feel-good" stuff in this chapter. Indeed, gratitude helps you feel good. It also helps you find purpose and fosters a greater connection to life within, around, and beyond.

And, if you're currently in the midst of a 911, I'd be willing to bet that very little of what you've just read actually landed.

I get it. Living in gratefulness for all of life's expressions and unfoldings is not easy. Though it's understandably more enjoyable to be imbibed with love-based emotions, of equal importance is the ability to tend to the painful emotions you experience in daily life, and especially in a 911.

Until we learn to navigate *all* emotions, it can feel next to impossible to move through life with gratefulness. Growth involves coming into harmony with the depth of emotional experience that lives inside of you—the experience you are wired to have.

It's okay if you haven't had extensive experience dealing with your emotions. Most people haven't. You may have been taught there are good and bad, right and wrong emotions. It makes sense, then, that you would employ various strategies to talk yourself out of emotions you deemed "not okay."

Yet, despite your best efforts to keep those emotions at bay (or maybe even "gratitude" them away), they found a way to make themselves known—internally, through Body, Mind, and Heart; and externally, by spilling out through reactive words and actions that cause further distress and suffering for you or someone else.

This act of allowing, honoring, and navigating the range of emotions that arise in our life is brand-new territory for many of us. In our pleasure-seeking, pain-avoidant society, we've been taught to deny, control, avoid, distract, or numb anything that does not feel good. Even during times of greater ease, its common to shove down inconvenient emotions to *keep it all together.*

It is no wonder, then, that there is often such a disconnect between people's public personas—the faces they believe are acceptable to show the world—and their true, private experience. Most of us live in this dichotomy to some extent. During times of stress, you may feel inadequate, or like a fraud or failure, because *everyone else* seems to have it all together. Or, you may fear backlash from others who are misusing emotion in hurtful ways (i.e., using emotional manipulation to get people to do what they want them to do).

Complicating matters are the multiple depths of emotion that live inside you. Some, you are well aware of—especially during a crisis, when heightened emotions are front and center. These are *known* emotions; there is no denying their presence and their impact on your outlook, mood, nervous system, and daily function. Yet there are also more subtle, subconscious-level emotions built up in your body from years of tamping down uncomfortable feelings. Typically, the day-to-day impact of these is less pronounced (at least, initially). These aches, tight shoulders or other impacts in the body are attributed to your daily grind—that is, until a tipping point occurs.

This unresolved emotional buildup is the result of years of pushing down emotions related to disappointments, dreams gone sideways, unfilled expectations, unachieved goals, regrets, slights, or betrayals. In the moment when these events occurred, you likely thought, *Now is not the right time to deal with this discomfort*, or feared that if you allowed *any* emotion to arise, too much would spill out, and no good would come from that. Maybe you were taught to "suck it up," or that "this, too, shall pass." Suffice to say that, for whatever reason, it is common to not process how you felt at the time. This energy however does not just go away. The body remembers, and creates an archive in your tissues to be referenced later.

I never really thought about the unexpressed emotion and grief I had left untended over the years until it made itself known in the most surprising way. While I was in grad school, I was invited to a party at my boss's house. I watched the interaction between him and his young daughter as he lovingly taught her how to make rice. He then asked me if I knew how to make rice—which I did not (hey, no judgment, friend)—and he taught me how to prepare this masterpiece with the same care. We proceeded to have a lovely evening. However, when I arrived home, I just started crying, and couldn't stop for hours. I was perplexed.

As I unpacked what the heck was going on, I realized that I was grieving the relationship I hadn't had with my own father. I always loved my dad and felt loved in return. Still, he wasn't the kind of role model or teacher-type dad depicted on Father's Day cards. I never really counted on him. I did learn a lot from him—some qualities I wanted to emulate and others I absolutely did not want to repeat—yet I had few memories of moments like the one I'd witnessed between my boss and his child, and part of me desperately wanted more.

That's what's happens when you don't know how to process emotional responses while they are occurring. They build up—and then, one day, boom! Your Soul says, "It's time." Time to grieve. Time to tune into the emotional energy stored in this earthly container. Your body was not designed to hold all of this, and a part of you is seeking this freeing release so you can move forward.

If this has happened (or is happening) to you, it's important to not make yourself wrong. No amount of judgment, blame, or shame will lead to emotional healing and freedom. Few of us were ever taught to view emotions as messengers, or as energies that can (and will) change and shift. The art is to honor the range as neither good or bad, and instead acknowledge what is and give those emotions a healthy outlet of expression—even if it's decades after the event itself.

The degree and intensity of emotional pain associated with your 911 will be unique to you. What is life-altering to one person may be practically routine to another. Your support system, finances, access to resources, and mental and physical health all play a role—as do the number of life-changing implications co-occurring, the meaning you've previously assigned to other challenging life experiences, your coping skills, and whether you have a belief in something greater than you.

How you handle pain will also depend on whether you are conditioned to "lash in" or "lash out." Lashing in is when you internalize over-responsibility for what is unfolding, whether it's yours or not. You might replay a scene in your mind over and over again, berating yourself for what you *should have* said or done, and then feel shame or blame. You likely don't share much about your struggles with others; it's held tightly inside. Many think you are a rockstar and move through life with ease and grace—yet, they have no idea that you're living with continual disappointment or self-loathing. On the contrary, there are those who tend to lash out—who have so much unprocessed emotional energy that when they are angry, upset, or overwhelmed they unconsciously dump it onto others. Often, this comes across as overreaction, as the trigger for lashing out may have little or nothing to do with events happening in the present moment.

To help you move through and beyond the suffering, it may be essential to do the very thing that you don't want to do and draw close what you would rather avoid. Specifically, draw close the emotional pain, and be with it as you would a child or a close friend. Get to know it. Appreciate it. Be tender with it. Wrap love around it. Then, ask the emotion, "What do you have to share?" When you truly listen, Body and Heart will help you tune into what is needed so you can help your body start releasing this trapped energy.

This takes courage and a big dose of self-compassion, yet it's essential to moving through your 911. Remember, emotions are energy. They are not *you*. You are the awareness aware of the discomfort or rawness of a particular emotion. Moving into and through the pain can be like learning how to be the stillness in the eye of the storm, and know it is possible. With practice, you can learn to honor what arises without letting it run the show.

It's important to note that embracing and working with your emotions in this way doesn't make your felt experiences any less real. It's okay to not feel okay right now. Sometimes, things suck. They hurt. You want them to stop. However, if you fear your emotions and refuse to tune into their narrative within Body and Heart, they invariably will take a toll on your well-being, quality of relationships, or life experiences.

There is freedom, wisdom, inner peace, and a whole bunch of goodness on the other side of emotional agility and nurturance. When you free up what's stored in your body, your heart can open, and your Soul can soar. Light and dark, all emotions play a vital role in growth. Test and try and be open to what you learn. And if you don't feel safe in releasing what is stored inside you on your own, I encourage you to find a supportive friend or an aligned, qualified professional who can support you in this process.

Nature *and* Gratitude

If you are feeling fearful, and have forgotten the strength that lies within, look to Nature to remind you of your nature.

Nature teaches us that all things shift, grow, change, and dissipate. There are high tides, low tides, and tides in between. All living beings are folded into a larger body of support. Even tsunamis eventually retreat into calmer water.

The feast of life is available and at the ready. It's been there all along—though perhaps you've have been too darn busy to notice it. One day before my "Nature Date," my mind was jampacked with agendas for the day ahead, the upcoming week, and the next decade. As the time came for me to step out of my to-dos, I lamented the lists not completed, the boxes not ticked off, and all that could go haywire while I pranced about in the woods and hugged trees like a wood nymph.

And yet, once I got out of my usual habitat, it was easier to shift my intention. I immersed in the gorgeous canvas of sky and land, and ... boom. The handiwork of nature, all the loving details of life, the innumerable renderings of the sacred right in front of me, all became visible. Alive. Real.

Enveloped in captivating beauty, time stood still. Vivid colors and patterns danced in wildflowers and wispy straw grass, while the meadow came alive with sparkling sun diamonds. As I was drawn into this wonder, the rhythm of my breath grew smoother; no longer was it harried or rushed. My heart rate slowed, soothing my mind. I became increasingly aware of what I noticed. Each piece of the whole was a message, an expanded perception of life in concert.

Holy wow.

Gratitude flooded my body. I went from feeling overwhelmed and uninspired to alive and grateful in the span of a few moments. Its rather remarkable how quickly our feelings can shift—and how, when they do, a tangible next right action just appears.

On those days when my body is full of messenger emotions vying for attention, I share my fears and grievances with my wise tree friends while anchored in the steadiness of the stones.

I whisper to Nature, *"I am willing to see this differently."*

I rest. I listen. I cry at times. I exhale the worry into an atmosphere of love.

And what I was holding on to so tightly suddenly becomes weightless.

In Nature, I talk to my emotions as if they have a voice. I imagine them imbued with sunlight and gently floating away with no effort on my part. I exhale tension and breathe in calm.

Practices

Intend, Immerse, Infuse

- *Intend:* Set an intention to be "in" the various moments of your day—to be truly present, and notice with child-like eyes filled with awe and wonder.
- *Immerse:* Each encounter holds a message and an offering.
    - When you are with other people, listen and observe with a beginner's mind, as though you had never met. We listen differently to strangers

than we listen to those we know well. What are the wisdom bits life is imparting to you through this person or the dialogue?

- If you are in Nature, drink in whatever catches your attention. That caterpillar you just stepped over on the sidewalk—where in your life might there be a transition or positive change arising for you? The stream flowing with ease as you stroll by—is there a project or relationship where following flow may be of greater value than pushing upstream to you?

- When you are at home, engage in an everyday activity with wonder. If you're eating, ask, "How many people made this meal possible?" Send appreciation to all known and unknown helpers, the people, the land, and your higher power (if that is part of your belief system).

- Transition mindfully between every activity. After you finish a meeting at work or a call with a friend, say, "This is complete." Then, as you begin the next moment, say, "I am here now."

- *Infuse:* Let life become more and more vibrant and alive. When you are present to it, life will offer thousands of opportunities to appreciate it. It will spark ideas, and remind you of the miracles that envelop you on a daily basis. Give thanks to your life, and share that gratitude forward.

Tune in, Honor, Release

This exercise will help you give voice to your emotions and create a pathway for release.

- Center through your breath. Breathe in through your nose and feel your belly expand. Then, breathe out through your mouth with a big, audible sigh. Engage in several rounds of this nurturing, rebalancing breath.

- Ground your body. Tap your feet on the floor and feel connected to the Earth. Or put your hands palm-down on your knees and notice the terrain of your kneecaps.

- Close your eyes. Scan your body for where emotional buildup or pain is taking up residence. For example, guilt can feel like a heaviness in your chest or gut. Anxiety might feel like a tightness around your lungs. Overwhelm might feel like tight knots in your shoulders. If you are unsure—if you hurt all over, or feel numb—ask your body where it hurts, keep breathing, and see if a particular area of your body comes to mind. If not, no worries; this can take practice.

- Become aware of the pain, remembering that you are the awareness, not the pain. Observe lovingly, as you would for your best friend.

- See your breath traveling to where it hurts (emotionally or physically) and expanding the space around it so that the trapped emotions can breathe, too. This might feel unsettling, as if the pain will get bigger—and it might for a while. Keep breathing and stay firmly grounded, knowing that you are the awareness.

- As you breathe, ask questions of the pain, such as: "What would you like me to know? What do you have to say? What do you need?" You can ask or offer anything you want in a loving, compassionate way.

- Offer comfort. This can be as simple as repeating, "I'm here. I care. I am listening."

- You may feel tears streaming, or you may yawn or feel a surge of a particular emotion. Offer yourself kindness, comfort, and reassurance.

- Envision a line of light streaming into the area. Breathe this light in through your whole body, as we did in Chapter 7. Then, direct the light to the source of the pain. See the pain enveloped in this loving light. Let bubbles of light soften the heavy density of the emotion. Then, imagine the light-bubbles carrying the emotion easily out of your body.

- Breathe steadily until your body tells you it's time to conclude the practice. Fill your heart with gratitude for your body, your emotions, and the wisdom of both.

- Whatever messages you discerned related to the emotions—integrate that wisdom as you move forward.

- On a regular basis, be with your body and attune to all the ways your body is speaking to you via emotions (mentally or physically). Remember, emotions are not right or wrong; rather, they are a form of communication to assist you as you navigate the fullness of life.

Just as it is not healthy to avoid painful emotions, it's also not healthy to be in them for hours. If you are feeling very raw or tender, I encourage you to time-bind this practice (i.e., engage for only five or ten minutes at a time). Start small and purposefully transition out of the practice when the time is up, thanking your body for its wisdom. Let it know, "I'll be back again." Afterwards, drop into the Spiritual Heart where you can anchor in peace. Consistent, smaller practices allow you to honor and release emotions, and bring Body back into harmony as you rest in your true nature.

Note: If you don't feel ready or safe to work with the energy of emotion in this way, there are a plethora of other options to empower you to tend to your embodied emotions. Journaling can give your emotions a voice and move them from your head onto a page. Moving your body through dance, yoga, or other practices can shake loose jammed emotions. You can even scream out loud in a car, or in nature when no one is around. Tapping (EFT), watching movies that help you emote, getting a massage, painting, playing music, energy healing, and talk therapy are also beneficial ways to meet, process, and release emotional energy. You do you; be willing to test and try.

Becoming Grateful

This chapter is an invitation to develop or further refine the art of living with gratefulness.

Ultimately, gratitude is a gateway for, and of, love. Through love, kindness, empowerment, connection, grace, wisdom, creativity, beauty, forgiveness, compassion, expansion, and resilience are born.

Gratefulness is not meant to cover up or cancel out raw emotions. Rather, it helps you find harmony in both delight and pain. Remember, emotions are not who we really are, though all shape our human experience. As we stand in the wholeness of our true nature, we can meet the range of human happenings.

Amanda now lives with a fire in her belly. While she's busy pursuing her dream role helping to connect people with stable housing, she deliberately pauses throughout her day to reflect upon the small moments with great appreciation. She now has greater trust in life and in her Spiritual Heart. These practices of Soul-aligned living and gratitude are new for her, yet she is beginning to clearly see how the events that shaped her early years are the very things that inspire her great drive and compassion. Though her new role comes with fewer material rewards than her old one, she finds that by giving her time, love, and energy, she feels fully alive. The rewards of being connected to a mission she believes in and people she cares about are beyond measure.

"What I thought was all wrong," she told me, "ended up being more right than I could have ever imagined."

Each experience was an essential stepping stone.

I can see clearly now.

It wasn't by accident.

Rather by intelligent design.

One I helped shape.

I embrace life in all its fullness,

and rest in the knowing that all serves.

Chapter 9

Service

I live in Service to life, and life is in service to me.

"**I** lost myself ..."

Lela lived her life as if life was solely about achievement.

That wasn't really the plan, but life just seemed to get away from her. How did the time pass so quickly? Of course, there was that one high school summer when she worked in Grand Canyon National Park—but that was impractical. Her early teachings were clear: get a good, sensible job that pays well, save your pennies, and keep climbing the ladder.

Besides, she reasoned, working in a park wasn't *really* a pathway to her dream life.

Fast forward twenty years. Lela had risen to a significant leadership role with a major retailer. Yet she felt no real connection to the company or its mission. In fact, when she really thought about it, the company and its products ran totally counter to her concerns regarding the environment and humanity's impact on it. During the week, she was usually too busy to think about it much—still, sometimes, while out on her "weekend warrior" hikes in the hills, that early experience around caretaking Nature haunted her like a ghost in the walls. Then, Monday would come, and it would be back to the grind.

Life was speaking to Lela, however her mind was still directing the show. She wasn't fully connected with the messages her Soul was sending through those memories.

She had a career, a very good one, though it felt disconnected with a deeper calling. She hadn't planned to be here; she'd just followed what felt like the next logical step. Now, those plans felt like they were unraveling. She was restless. Longing.

When we started working together, she agreed to take small steps toward cultivating a new relationship with life. Rather than starting her day with diving into emails and calls, now she gets quiet and listens. Having grown up in an agnostic family, she had very little relationship with the idea of a higher power. Yet, she acknowledged that life seemed to be pretty intelligent (when she stopped to think about it). It was enough to open the doorway.

The more Lela allowed herself to not "figure everything out," the more life seemed to keep unfolding for her. At the time, she couldn't make sense of what was happening; still, she committed to trusting in the moments that life and Soul spoke to her, and to do her best to listen and trust those nudges.

During this time, a big, rather unexpected event occurred. Lela had intended to stay married to her one love forever, and to become a mother through that union. It was her ideal plan, but he had fallen out of love. "You have lost the wonder of life," her former partner told her. When they'd first met, she had been consumed by the beauty of the world, spending joyful time with her lover and friends and appreciating nature. Although it pained her greatly to hear this, his words rang true. Over the years, she'd lost herself in work and ambition—and sacrificed joy for commitments that, in hindsight, had been obligatory, not inspired.

After the divorce, she decided she needed to get away from it all. She planned a solo hike abroad—her first in decades. There, walking the land, enveloped by breathtaking beauty, she remembered what it was like to feel alive. She left a trail of tears and giggles, joys and regrets, through the mountains and down to the ocean.

"How did I lose myself in the process of trying to make a life for myself?" She asked in one of our sessions.

"You are not alone; it is actually very common," I replied. "I am glad you're here now. Although you feel lost, the answers and path are closer than it may seem."

Upon returning from her sabbatical, Lela reconnected with the mission of her company in a significant way. She decided to take her passion for environmental activism and become an advocate for change within her organization. She found that she could serve the mission while also working to expand it on both a process level and a consciousness level. Now, she wakes up with "juice" in her body, heart, and Soul again.

Her dream of becoming a mother hasn't come to fruition in the way she envisioned. Yet, she has absolutely birthed something new through her work, and is finding it deeply fulfilling and rewarding. And the more she connects to her natural *joie de vivre,* pays attention to the flow of her life, spends time in nature, and connects with the people around her, the more wondrous and fulfilling life becomes. Most of all, she designs her day by listening, chooses her yeses more carefully, and puts joyful service ahead of obligation.

What *is* Service?

Ah, yes. The progressive journey.

"Know thyself," Plato wrote. How profound this wisdom and invitation is for us all. Yet this is not a one-and-done task, as your true nature is ever-unfolding. Every step of the way, life is moving you—or moving through you—in service to you, and to life.

I would never have chosen the path I've walked on my own. Of course, my choices and consequences played a role, and an important one. Yet, there was always something bigger going on—something bigger than my vision and understanding, and more intentional that anything my mind could have plotted.

In most cases, the "something bigger" wasn't visible or understandable until much later in the journey. Each experience, regardless of how good (or awful) it felt at the time, was an essential springboard leading to the next iteration of my becoming. I did not know, and could not have envisioned, how the collective moments of my life could be stitched together to create a blooming web of growth and realization.

If not for my unique life experiences, I would not be who I am today. Without your unique life experiences—including your current 911—you would not be who you have become. We have evolved *by design*.

No matter how little they make sense in this now moment, your life experiences are not random, accidental, or pointless. They do not take place in isolation. Each moment you live, each encounter, each conversation, is purposeful—an invitation to give and receive, to learn or stagnate, to hold on or let go. The universe does not waste moments.

Each Soul, including yours, has a path. Your experience is always in service to your highest truth and potentiality in some way. Your life is the path to discovering and living that truth in all the ways that serve you, and life, more broadly.

Your key moments, synchronicities, and critical 911 inflection points present on both individual and collective levels. Sometimes they are subtle and slow; other times, they take place in an instant.

The global pandemic of 2020 was a collective 911 that led many of us to personal 911s. Ignoring the situation, or wishing it away, was not an option for anyone. Although many were better protected by privilege, wealth, or status, all of us felt the impact of it at some level. From an Earth View, the pandemic (and the ensuing lockdowns) brought death, illness, fear, economic wreckage, separation, division, and distrust.

Systems at all levels—including political, healthcare, police, education, and financial systems—revealed their vulnerabilities, under-preparedness, racial biases, and inherent prejudices. All the things we took for granted were suddenly up for examination.

In short, it became very apparent to all of us that a return to "normal" was not only impossible but hugely counterproductive. Now that we know what "normal" actually entails, it is no longer the kind of world we, as a collective, want to live in.

From Soul View, this collective 911 was an invitation to clear division, anger, and separation. To focus more deeply inward, reconnect with loved ones and nature, and create more of what we truly value. To live with greater clarity, intention, purpose, and gratitude for everything and everyone around us. To create something new for the good of all.

Knowing that this was a global call to action for the good of all does not negate the pain, upheaval, loss, and suffering of this time. The seeds of wisdom were planted at a tremendous human cost. From a Soul View perspective, the magnitude of the tragedy makes it even more important that we follow the path being presented to us. We must make the fundamental changes life is requesting—no, *demanding*—of us, regardless of whether they are convenient, fun, or easy.

Whether a 911 is individual or collective, Soul knows the way. What you've learned thus far in this book has taught you to tune in, listen, receive guidance, and to trust the wisdom of Soul, Heart, and life. Now, it's time to see how this comes to life with service.

THE EARTH VIEW OF SERVICE

The clients I partner with are highly committed to service.

What service means to them professionally in large part is informed by the what, how, and why. The what is the value proposition of a service (or set of services) for the organization. The how is how they will bring the vision of service to life. And the why is the reason the service matters to the company, the intended beneficiaries, and themselves.

On the personal side, my clients have clear ideas and intentions regarding what it means to provide love, support, and the desired quality of life for their family, loved ones, or community of choice.

They also fall into the "I have to make it happen" camp with regard to service. They operate largely from what is visible, tangible, and actionable. They often go to exhausting lengths to organize, plan, and strategize the delivery of the company mission while simultaneously creating their personal meaning and outcomes. They have a fierce sense of independence which has served them well, yet also increases the level of pressure they feel to take responsibility for things they cannot control. They've been prone to sacrifice their time, their relationships, and even their health because they feel that, if they relax too much, life might snatch away everything they've worked for.

They deliver again and again, because they know that their contributions matter to a whole lot of people (as well as to them personally). This reflects their high sense of integrity and desire to achieve with excellence.

However, when I ask them, "How do you live in service to life?" I'm usually met with a pause, and a reflection. Sometimes, there's a recoil.

If you also recoiled at the idea of being "in service" to life, maybe you feel that life only moves when you personally take control and *force* it to move. Or, maybe you feel like you've been a victim to life's careless, cruel whims, and now have to operate in "damage control" mode. Either way, to be in service to a faceless, nameless force that may or may not care about you might (depending on your beliefs) seem like an implausible stretch or an outright joke.

The second part of the principle—"and life is in service to me"—might be easier to buy into if life is going well for you right now. Maybe things are turning out exactly as you hoped, and you can see a pathway toward what you want. But when life throws you a curveball, this notion of service is likely to be met with skepticism, anger, despair, or just, "You've got to be kidding me!" Your prayers were not answered. Your plans were shredded. You *did everything right* (or mostly right); therefore, this latest experience is unfair, wrong, and just plain crappy.

When you insist that life does what you want it to, you remove life, and all its vast intelligence, from the equation. Rarely do we get a glimpse of the "master plan"—and so, when we strive for control, we make decisions with a narrow sliver of information according to a limited Earth School viewpoint. Is it any wonder that sometimes life has a good giggle about that?

Gratefully, life is in service to you.

You are a good person, doing good work, trying your best

to live a good life. Yet it's also possible that, in the daily whirl-wind, you have simply lost your connection to all of the small and infinitely beautiful ways in which life is serving you every day. Even if you have a gratitude practice, you may not be well-versed in this kind of thinking. It's often only when the gift and the privilege of being served feels like it's been taken away that we notice it at all.

Our beliefs about life—what it is, what it means, what it does—are anchored in the idea of linear time. We understand that we have a past, that we are living in the present, and that we have a future. In that context, the idea that we don't actually know who we are, where we are going, or why it all matters feels … unacceptable. Those who are wrestling with these questions often during a 911 are judged, labeled, and even shamed. If they "had it together," Earth School wisdom says, they would be in a different place. And so, even as we struggle with the immensity of the not-knowing, we blame ourselves for not knowing. It's vicious, and totally counter to life's positive intentions for us.

At the core of this struggle to accept life's service to us is our innate feeling of separation. We view ourselves as separate from life. Separate from other people, in terms of beliefs, race, income, education, health, religion, gender, or something else. Separate from what's unfolding in the lives of others, whether across the street or across the world. Separate, even, from our own souls. All of our current power structures are built upon this separateness, and "us versus them" is so common in our discourse that we simply accept it as true. We don't feel responsible for all, but rather for ourselves (and those of our choosing) because we feel like islands in a vast, unpredictable sea of local and global events.

Accepting that life is in service to us means, above all, accepting that *we are not separate*—not from life, and not from one another. If every person who comes into your world is sent by life to convey some meaning, some lesson, or some experience to you—or to be given some meaning, lesson, or experience through you—then we *cannot* be entirely separate. This line of thinking crosses into highly spiritual territory, which can be uncomfortable or even unbelievable for those of us used to operating in a logical, linear space.

I don't expect that this new view will take root for you right away—or at all. That is up to you to discern for yourself. Test and try. Ask yourself, "If I knew that life was unfolding in service to me, how would I think about things differently?" As you sit in stillness, see what your Heart, Body, and Soul have to say about this line of questioning. Stay open and listen. This is next-level growth in your Earth School journey.

Over the course of our journey through this book, you've been invited to explore what most of us have not been taught: how to garner wisdom from, and move in flow with, life. There is greater opportunity, expanded potentiality, alignment, and joy on offer when we stop trying to force a desired outcome from life through struggle or pushing against the natural current. You are not an independent agent bearing the weight of the world on your shoulders; rather, you are part of a universe of creative agents who are always at the ready to assist you.

The more you make time to tap into your expanded wisdom (versus relying on fear-based Mind), anchor in faith and trust, and consider service in a greater context, the more you will begin to see the myriad ways in which you are serving life, and life is serving you.

THE SOUL VIEW OF SERVICE

Have you ever asked, "Life, how would you like me to serve?"

Who you are, and the roles you play in your daily existence, makes a big impact on the collective. Whether you show up as your best self or your crankiest, your most aligned and excited or your most despairing, creates a ripple that influences everything in your orbit and the greater orbit. You matter, and who you are being matters.

Have you ever had a moment where something totally unexpected came flying out of your mouth? Maybe something that felt harsh, or "too much"—and then, the recipient came back days later and said, "What you said really got me thinking. Those words changed my life." Yep, that's life working through you. And when you shift into the Soul View of service and put yourself in a place of serving life with joy, these kinds of synchronistic moments will happen more and more often.

Unfortunately, many of us aren't taught as children to serve life, and to let life serve others through us, in this way.

Growing up, I had hardworking parents and extended family who served many people. Mom was a nurse. Dad owned a restaurant and did odd jobs. One set of grandparents owned a hardware store, while the others were dairy and grain farmers. They all served, and served well—and they were always there when someone needed a helping hand. At the same time, their service was a practical means to an end. It put food on the table and a roof over our heads. There was no discussion of, or understanding around, the impact of our actions in any global sense. You worked hard, you served, you came home, you gave thanks, you did it again. (This way of understanding service was consistent for most in that era, as the internet was not a reality, and world connectivity and impact was not yet understood locally or globally.)

In my earlier career, I followed that same model. I served through my work, and that service created an outcome. I often asked, "How can I deliver the highest value and best possible outcome here?" but I never thought to ask, "How does life want me to serve here?" For decades, I thought I understand the law of action and effect; however, I never truly connected the dots on the systemic impact of my choices—particularly with regard to my consumption patterns and buying patterns, and the often-destructive systems and practices I was unknowingly and inadvertently endorsing with those choices.

The Soul View of Service is about taking responsibility for our true place in the web of life, and letting life guide us to the inflection points where we can do the most good, in alignment with our purpose and truth.

You are an extraordinarily powerful creator. And you do not create in a void. You create as part of an ever-shifting whole, to which you constantly contribute meaning, energy, and movement. When you consciously make the choice to serve life, the path is eased. Rather than giving up your autonomy, you liberate yourself. By living in service to life, you become totally alive and aligned—and a change agent who helps to uplift humanity.

Isn't that delicious?

Imagine a life shaped both by the intelligence coded within you—Body, Mind, and Heart—and by Soul, life, and the Divine itself. All in service: for you, and through you. What would that look like? Feel like? What would be different?

The surrender into service does require one sacrifice. It requires you to go beyond your ego. You have a powerful role to play, and there is also a grander plan in place that is beyond you and your control (you have free will, and there are unfoldings outside of free will)—and that master plan is evolving daily. Anchored in love, fueled by divine imagination, you can both fulfill all you came here to be and collectively co-create a new expression of heaven on Earth.

Yes, that's really the plan: for all of us to live in harmony, peace, prosperity, and joy. Any 911, individual or collective, is a launchpad on that path. It's a reconfiguration of "reality" to match what life, and Soul, really desires for us. And in that new reality, we can be who we truly are, without the filters, meanings, biases, and limitations that have covered up our truth and made us forget our true essence.

Life speaks of this plan to you every day—through joy and sorrow, laughter and tears. All moments. Every happening. Each sign and symptom. Each pain. Each joy. Every encounter.

Every opportunity seized, and every opportunity missed. Each is a teacher of great value, if only you are willing to listen, discern the wisdom, and integrate the lesson in service to self, others, and the world.

THE BEAUTY OF THE "AND"

Soul understands that, sometimes, incredibly sad things happen—and that, ultimately, some greater good will be served. When you are in struggle or being challenged, you are not being punished, and you have not been forgotten. And though there may never—from a human perspective—be a "reason" capable of justifying the loss and suffering, from a Soul View, the loving truth will reveal itself in time. Divine consciousness plays the long game. Knowing this can be incredibly helpful, however that doesn't take away, nor is it intended to invalidate, the searing pain you may be in now. Both can be simultaneously true.

We have all witnessed the love paid forward by those who have weathered unspeakable acts. They become voices of change, leaders of movements, beacons of light. They understand what those who have not walked in that kind of darkness can never fathom.

In Soul View, you honor the "and" of being fully human—including pain and grief that is very real and life-changing—and fully divine—resting in an understanding fully connected to Soul and Heart beyond the rational mind. You release the need to understand the "why" of things, for you know you cannot. Rather, you are invited to expand your view, surrender into love and the compassion always available for you from within, and dwell in the wonder of it all.

I'm sure you can think of a time in your life where everything felt like a disaster in the moment—nevertheless, when you look back, you can honestly say, "Thank goodness I didn't get my way!" That college you didn't get into, that relationship that ended before you were ready, that job that fell apart, that health scare that changed everything … all of these things opened doors that led to something better than you could have imagined from where you were standing then. Despite your insistence, a bigger plan prevailed, for which you are now grateful.

This is the "and" of Service. We are in service to life, and life is in service to us. We are human and divine. We are creators, and we are guided. And we are, all of us, in the process of that holy reassembly: we are finding our way home to ourselves.

The invitation here is to reimagine your life and its purpose from an aerial Soul View. You are invited to become aware of the meanings you assign to life and all its various aspects: things, people, places, feelings, events, etc. Heck, you can even examine your thoughts about the weather, or that funny look the barista gave you last time you ordered your two-thirds-de-caf-mocha-latte-with-oat-milk-but-yes-please-whipped-cream. None of it means anything until you decide it does—and the meaning you decide on depends entirely on your perspective.

Summon the willingness to suspend all of your current meanings. Be in stillness, and arrive at a view unclouded by judgments, filters, and fear. Ask for Soul and Heart to illuminate what you are experiencing, and give you instructions as for how to proceed. Ask questions like, "If this was all unfolding in service to me, how would I see it differently?" or simply, "What is this reflecting to me?" The nature of your questions will significantly influence what you see, hear, feel, and do next; the answers you receive are important, however your availability to open and wonder are essential and where it begins.

Create solitude and hold yourself in the questions for a while. Whatever feelings arise, let them come. Be compassionate and loving to yourself first and foremost—especially if you're scared that you've made a big mistake, can't see a way out, or feel betrayed by life in some way. Surrender the need to know it all, and know it now, and anchor in the wisdom of Heart. It takes courage to walk into the unknown with nothing except a loving trust in life's goodness and confidence in the knowing lens of Soul's wisdom—yet this is the dance of being fully human, and fully eternal.

If the present feels muddled or overwhelming, turn the lens of this Soul View of Service toward your history for context. What patterns or experiences have called you to healing and evolution? How were those patterns an invitation to become more of who you came here to be? What might be some of the Earth School curriculum you signed up for?

A treasure trove of insight awaits you when you make space for this level of inquiry. Simultaneously, there is zero pressure to come up with some profound insight, or to use your new relationship with the past to map out the future in exquisite detail. If we try too hard to come up with solutions, those solutions are likely to be suboptimal. The wisdom you need right now will arise. The rest will save itself for when the time is right.

If you found this book, chances are you've already spent a fair amount of time reviewing your history through many modalities and with various providers. If you have not done this work or are inclined to go deeper in your review of your life experiences, I recommend partnering with a trained professional versed in the kinds of experiences you've been through, particularly with regard to trauma.

Meanwhile, in your day to day, the best way to live in the beauty of the "and" is to consciously invest the majority of your vision, energy, thoughts, and actions into aligning with what you desire to create. Go big—bigger than what seems possible or plausible. While the past holds interesting insights and answers relative to that context (and somewhat for today's state), the future is being created out of the *now*. Forgive yourself for yesterday's transgressions and today's mistakes. Do that often, as most of us are way too hard on ourselves. Hold it all loosely, anchor in your values, and stay open and curious. Remember that what is true *is true at this point in time*, and is therefore subject to change. Endeavor to live in a way that aligns with and perpetuates what you desire—both for yourself and the collective—and trust that life always has your back.

Working *with* Service

You were not born into a vacuum. Rather, you entered the web of life—an energetic grid which has ancestral, cultural, local, and global context.

Being born is, in some ways, like starting a new job. When you walk through those doors on your first day, you enter into a complex system of the company's pre-existing beliefs, norms, politics, and relationships. You have a role with associated responsibilities. It's not a blank canvas, ever; even in a startup, each human being brings all of their beliefs, preferences, biases, experiences, perceptions, meanings, etc. to the table. Such is the case when you are born onto this planet, into a family.

You are born as the pure essence of love and potentiality, however there is a process of undoing we all go through, both visibly and invisibly, as souls in a human expression. To come back to who you truly are, and discern the true nature and scope of your role here on Planet Earth, you need to be willing to unlearn what you have learned, refine your philosophies, theories, and certainties, and embrace what is true for you at a Soul level.

Soul knows the way. We also can't rush Soul's timing. Like a baby's birth, or the emergence of a butterfly from its cocoon, there is an intelligence in creation which involves timing we don't dictate. We cannot demand our Soul's growth to suit our preferences. When we try to speed things up, get to the gold, and move on to the good stuff, we are operating from ego and not from Soul, and life will intervene to set us right. Sometimes, we simply are not ready until we are ready—and because life is always unfolding for our greatest good, we will never miss out on what is meant for us.

I invite you to pause for a few moments and reflect on one specific aspect of your life. That might be your current job, your relationship, the home or location you live in, or a major turning point in your life. What are some of the stepping stones that led you along the path to this place in your life? Was there a moment when you received a suggestion or piece of information from someone that led you to look where you otherwise may not have? Was the job you have now made possible because of a past role that helped you develop certain skills (even if you didn't know why you were building those skills at the time)? Did the end of one relationship clear the way for even richer love? Where has life moved you in a direction that fundamentally supported the next evolution of *you*?

Be with the wonder of this. We often feel such immense pressure to "get it right," make the best decision, or figure everything out ahead of time. Yet, the whole time, life is guiding and supporting us. There is an orchestration we cannot see or know. Yes, we are called to show up as our highest self and keep learning and growing in Earth School. And, at the same time, we get to relax and trust that life, and Soul, have a bigger plan.

Just like reading, writing, and arithmetic are core curricula for students in school, we all have a core curriculum in Earth School. I Am Enough 101. I Am Love 101. I Belong 101. These are the mandatory courses—and until we learn the associated lessons, life will lovingly present us with experiences that support the required lessons. You may also get to take special "electives" like Boundary Setting, Assertiveness, Speaking Your Truth, or Work/Play Harmony, to name a few. I'll bet that with some thought you can readily identify the themes within your own curriculum for growth. And while these lessons may be difficult at the time, all are in service to your progressive journey.

Nature *and* Service

We share the same basic building blocks with all of life: the sun, the rocks, the trees. Nothing exists independently, and nothing exists for no reason.

It's rather remarkable how leaves, branches, and petals grow in spirals so that the new leaves don't block the sun from the older ones, and so the maximum amount of rainwater gets directed to the root systems. Each new expression emerges in service to those that came before.

The food chain is another beautiful expression of service. Each life form has a place in an endless cycle of service. The grass feeds the antelope, the antelope feeds the cheetah—and the cheetah, when its life is done, feeds the grass. None can exist without the others.

Even forest fires (when naturally occurring as prescribed burns) are in service to the whole. They clear debris and disease from the ground, crack open the seeds of the redwood giants, and make way for new life to emerge.

Nature reminds us to ask, "Are my patterns equally on purpose? Do they serve me, and serve life?" If not, your 911 might be handing you the opportunity for a life-giving burn. Even when intense fires rage, in time, and with tending, the ecosystem rebuilds. Nature has an amazing capacity to heal and adapt—and so do we.

In some cases, as with global climate shifts, what was once a perfect ecosystem is no longer functional, and is asked to adjust. How similar for us! What at one point in time was a perfect job, a perfect relationship, a perfect chance for us to serve, is no longer viable. When this happens, look to Nature for inspiration. Once the new conditions become clear, you are invited to plant new seeds, tend new ground, and grow something beautiful and unexpected.

Practices

A powerful way to tune into the principle of Service is to ask aligned questions. Some of these you may remember from the Mind chapter; now you are invited to journal about them through the lens of Service, and see what emerges.

- What is _____ reflecting to me?
- What is the invitation of _____?
- What is this shining a light on to heal or evolve beyond?
- What wants to be born in me?
- What wants to be born *through* me?
- How might _____ be in service?
- What does life want for me?
- What does life want through me?
- What do I want from life?

Living in Service

The principle of Service invites us into another level of truth. Not only is life in service to us, we are in service to it. The questions we ask shift from, "What can I get?" to "What can I give?"

Service is the highest path a Soul can walk, and opportunities to be of service to life are endless. Service is a dynamic exchange. As many wise teachers have said, giving is receiving. You don't need to devote yourself to grand gestures and worldwide initiatives if that's not your passion, or if it's impractical. Cooking with love, reading to kids or older adults, volunteering, deep listening, a smile for a stranger: all of these are profound acts of service, during which you can mindfully allow life to move through you.

Your life is a message. Service is how you let it sing.

Lela now feels the exquisite "and" of being in service to life, and life being in service to her. Through Soul-sight, she now connects the dots of various life experiences that have shaped who she is today and how she understands her greater nature. She was in awe as she recounted the many moments—full of people, places, chance happenings, immense joy and pain—that played a role in her ability to live fully, now.

Stillness has become a treasured ritual of connection with the invisible realm which she never thought existed. It informs how she moves through the day in more harmony with work and play, dedication and freedom. Her vision of environmental activism brought nature to the forefront of a company that had never considered such a path before. Nature is once again her playground; it is a reunion long foreshadowed in the dreams she previously dimmed.

"Maybe," she says now with a grin, "I was never really lost after all."

I AM Love empowered,

divinely infused,

cosmically supported,

the field of infinite possibility enlivened.

YES!

Chapter 10

I am Love, and say yes to leading with love.

"Why did it take me so long? Have I missed out on too much?" Those were Mary's words to me when, months after the finalization of her divorce, she still struggled to fill the void inside herself and feel complete outside of a relationship.

Despite growing up with parents who clearly loved her, Mary never felt worthy. Although she was supported and cheered on in her home, her school years were tough. She was often teased about her weight, and about "being weird." From a young age, she remembers feeling different than everyone else. To cultivate a feeling of "being enough," she poured herself into academic achievement.

She found her tribe in college—a group of friends she related to and felt like she belonged to. Yet, those early impressions of feeling unworthy, maybe even unlovable, were alive in her mind daily. She judged herself for every single thing she did or didn't do.

Her marriage played out those dynamics as well. Being with her (now ex) husband felt a lot like those childhood playgrounds, full of criticism and exclusion—which was why, initially, her divorce felt like a huge step toward freedom. The dissolution was her choice; she thought this ending would be just what she needed to create the *whole* life experience (personal and professional fulfillment and success) she craved. But breaking free hadn't disentangled her from those old feelings of "not enough"—in fact, they were louder than ever.

Struggling with shame, berating herself for "letting herself go," frustrated that her life plan wasn't staying at all on track, she was on an endless Ferris wheel of comparison and self-judgment. Plenty of other people her age had it all together, so why didn't she?

Outwardly, Mary was an incredibly successful entrepreneur. Those who worked with her marveled at her visionary capacity, passion, and willingness to be bold and take big risks. They assumed she must have unshakeable confidence and belief in herself. There was some truth to this perception; when it came to business, Mary repeatedly placed bets on herself and her big ideas. She had a gift for anticipating and solving customers' unmet needs—and her business success proved it.

Yet, the moment she set foot outside the "comfort zone" of her work environment—whenever she was alone, or when she needed to interact with unfamiliar people in new situations—

Mary's confidence and self-belief seemed to vanish. She often felt as though she were living two different lives.

Up until this point, Mary had been able to compartmentalize her doubt. Lately, though, the inner critic had become incessant, to the point where it was invading her business, too. She'd begun to question every choice she made, asking, "Why didn't I do this? Why did I say that? Why didn't I see this sooner? Why am I so far behind?"

And, of course, the most gut-wrenching question of all: "What is *wrong* with me?"

There were days when she wondered if life would have been better even if she'd stayed with her ex. Yes, he'd been judgmental, and immature, and not really reliable ... but he'd been better than no one. Now, it was just her—and she was having a very hard time living with herself.

Life, as it does, was presenting Mary with the exact opportunity to claim what she desired: to feel comfortable in her own skin and create the inner and outer life experiences she longed for. She was on a quest to align with a deeper truth of her nature, and to reclaim strength, power, and autonomy in all areas of her being. More, she was being offered a chance to truly love herself, flaws and all, while at the same time expanding her capacity to create a meaningful and fulfilling life—professionally *and* personally.

Little by little, Mary began to realize that she'd been playing small just about everywhere: in her marriage, in her family, with her passions and adventures, and even in her work (though no one looking at her from the outside would have said that).

She'd tried to fit the expansiveness of her true self into a box her husband could live with—and now, the box was tearing at the seams. She worried that she'd lost too many years living a half-life.

The thing about Soul growth is that you're ready when you're ready (even if you don't know you're ready). From the outset of our work together, Mary presented with openness, commitment, and a hunger for positive change. Her body had been a tightly-closed storehouse of self-loathing, shame, and sadness for years. The feelings of success at work could no longer override the parts of her seeking healing and integration. Through various practices—many of which are outlined in this book—she was able to process, honor, and find creative outlets for those energies.

Something rather miraculous happens when you align with Love and allow parts of your conditioned self to either fall away or meld in. Your body recognizes resonance instantly. You can trust its wisdom and abilities to heal itself.

Although Mary didn't at first believe the shifts in Mind that her Heart guided, she was a woman on a mission, and she followed Heart's counsel nonetheless. At first, tapping into Heart wisdom felt like a practice she scheduled; before long, however, it became a conscious way of living. Her weight—physically and metaphorically—has lifted. She has befriended her body.

Now, Mary has a fully integrated and fulfilling life. She is comfortable speaking her truth. She lives her preferences out loud and head on. Is she "weird"? No—and yes. Or maybe both. She doesn't care anymore. She has embraced her eccentricities, rejoined poetry and writing clubs, made Joy dates alone and with friends, and traveled abroad. The success once reserved for her business is now a felt experience in all of her life.

She has invited Love into her life. And she doesn't just glow; she *radiates*.

What *is* Love?

If you asked the profound, existential question, "Why are we here?" I would answer in one word: "Love."

You are here to liberate and free yourself from anything and everything that separates you from your true nature, which is Love. Your only *real* work in life is to release all false narratives, conditioning, and illusions of separateness that keep you from being Love, in all ways, all the time.

Love is your greatest superpower, and the greatest power in the world. There is no interaction that cannot benefit from loving presence, words, and actions. Love is your guide, your informant, and your companion on this crazy, beautiful path called life.

Love is also the greatest of the truths you are searching for. Your 911 has opened the door for you to see that, even if you weren't aware, you have been looking for Love in every part of your life—things, people, places, experiences. But this isn't Hollywood: you won't find the true, divine Love you seek in some idyllic relationship or situation. Rather, it is inside yourself. Beautiful, messy, imperfect, powerful, clumsy, gorgeous, human ... you are always, and only, Love.

Your 911 is, at its heart, a call for Love in your life. It offers an opportunity to embrace the empowered Source energy that you are, and are connected to. Simultaneously, it offers permission to be fully human, and open your human heart more fully to the experience of love in this life. Just like you, Love is finite and infinite.

And yet, very few of us live with this multi-faceted understanding of love. Even if we know that Love is what we're seeking, we get confused as to what Love actually is. We think it's external. Conditional. Available only at certain times, or if we meet very specific qualifications.

Most of us were also taught that love is good in your personal life, but not so much in business. It's too soft, to unpredictable. Too likely to change, evaporate, or revert into anger. To lead with love in a business setting at best sets you up for embarrassment, at worst for utter collapse. Love isn't something we build structures on.

Given that this is our starting point, is it any wonder Love gets mixed reviews (and some truly bad press)?

Real Love, Soul-led Love, is not like anything we have experienced or been taught. It's not superficial, transient, or situational. It doesn't require us, or others, to be "worthy" before we give and receive it. Rather, Love is whole and is already healed. It's the missing piece you've been yearning to find—maybe for your entire life, or maybe just since your 911 began.

Only when you remember the love you are can you realize that there was nothing to search for to begin with. Rather, your quest is, and has always been, about reuniting with the parts of you that you had left behind, and transmuting anything that is preventing your wholeness. It's the "sacred" in your search for the sacred, and the glue that will hold you in your holy reassembly.

What you need, what your loved ones need, what future generations need, and what the world needs, is *you*. You, as Love. You, fully expressed—with Soul, Mind, Body, Heart, Gratitude, and Service on board and harmonized.

THE EARTH VIEW OF LOVE

Wow, do we Earth-dwellers put up a fight around love.

On the one hand, we venerate love as The Solution to everything, the facilitator of happy endings, the force that overcomes all evil. On the other hand, we see love as destructive, maddening, unpredictable, capricious, and elusive. Often, we think it's something other people have but we don't.

The Earth View of Love is that love emerges from the emotional Heart. However, since many of our natural and conditioned human emotions are rooted in fear, scarcity, and confusion, those things attach themselves to Love and limit its potential.

For example, from a young age, we learn that saying and doing the "right" things will "get" us love from parents, siblings, caregivers, and friends. When we did certain things, we felt loved, so that state was associated in our minds as "lovable"—as if love was a reward. On the other hand, when we did something "wrong," love was withheld. Maybe we were even punished.

This patterning follows us into adulthood. Think for a moment about all you do, say, and strive for in the name of love. Maybe you worry about your physical appearance before going on a date, certain that you won't be "lovable" if you don't pass muster. Maybe you worry about how your performance at work will affect your peers' regard for you, and struggle with the feeling that one mistake could derail everything you've worked so hard to build. Maybe you hold yourself back from trying the new, adventurous things that your Heart desires because you don't want to risk looking clumsy or incapable—because who could love a dunce?

All around us are proscribed codes of worth and merit. They can look like the common dichotomies of right/wrong, holy/evil, smart/stupid, beautiful/ugly, hardworking/lazy, rich/poor, desirable/not desirable, successful/unsuccessful, etc.—but no matter how they're framed, what they really come down to is *worthy of love/unworthy of love.*

Love from a human perspective usually comes with limitations, conditions, and expiration dates. And yet, at the same time, we are all craving unconditional acceptance. We desire to love and be loved outside of our protective walls—and yet, we make it almost unbearably hard on ourselves to do either. Thus, the constant search for that undefinable "something missing."

Life is always a work in progress. Particularly when you're leading with ego, your progress often comes through adversity, or through a reaction to fear. Judgments abound about how you look, how you speak, what material "goodies" you have (or don't have), what titles and certifications you've earned (or haven't), what beliefs you have (or don't have), who your partner is (or isn't). We talk about righteousness and sin. Yet when you come down to it, each of these judgments is a biased rationale or excuse we employ to withhold and manipulate Love.

Sometimes, we buy into these judgments to "get" love; sometimes, we rely on them to "keep" love. We walk on eggshells for fear our beloveds will find out we don't fit neatly into the boxes anymore. Even when our jobs, our relationships, our friends, or our hobbies feel too small, too constraining, we tamp down our higher expression of our loving selves in deference to the status quo. Then, feeling strangled and small, we judge and withhold love from others who choose a different path. Or, like Mary, we withhold love from ourselves. We might even justify all of it through our cultural and religious lens of "rightness."

So, the cycle continues.

The most interesting part, though, is that through it all, almost none of us realize what we're actually doing. It all feels so normal; it's just "how the world works."

Only when, at some level, we decide to unhook ourselves from these Earth View-based judgments can we rise into a greater expression of who we are, and increase our bandwidth for love. Love requires us to go all in—to sort through the messy, false boundaries of our inner labyrinths that are keeping us separate from our true nature of Love.

As Marianne Williamson wrote, "All is love or a call to love."

The divisiveness we see playing out across the world today isn't a demonstration of right/wrong or any other dichotomy.

It's a symptom of withholding love, because, deep down, we collectively fear love and its power. The mechanisms of war, media, and even business as we know it would not stand up to unharnessed love.

And yet, as much as many of us desire Love, we can't will it. We can't make it happen; Love simply *is*. And regardless of the circumstances, it is always and only the way through.

As an ensouled being, you seek harmony. You seek a return to Love. You've seen the opposite; now, you're searching for the sacred truth. The greatest gift of feeling lost is the eventual finding of a new, better place. It's a curiosity, an awakening to what is possible outside of our well-traveled paths. It's an awakening to a new way of seeing, and *being*, Love.

THE SOUL VIEW OF LOVE

Spiritual Love is profoundly simple. It is the purest power in the universe. It is your true essence, eternal and perfect as your Soul. It is ever evolving, and yet unchanging and unwavering.

Imagine, for a moment, a love like that. A love that never falters, even when you make a really messy choice, leave a relationship, or challenge others' beliefs through your ensouled expression. A love that holds you when you step out of the box that so many can't even see. A love that exists beyond doubt. A love that heals what appears unhealable.

Spiritual Love is beyond the emotional Heart. It's different. Deeper. Rather than riding the waves of emotional highs and lows, it tempers them. Rather than bending to conditions, it transcends them. And yet, it's practical and steady in its provision of clarity, joy, and freedom.

The thirst to discover our true purpose is rooted in our search for Spiritual Love. We want to know we matter—and when we remember that we matter to Love, all other means of "mattering" become insignificant. We become less focused on qualifying for love from other humans, and more focused on living purposefully from moment to moment, knowing that we *are* Love.

Robert Holden taught that, "Love is intelligent." I could not agree more. Love has no form. It's invisible—and yet, I'll bet you can conjure up many examples of its tangible impact. Those times when you felt seen, heard, and like all of you was welcomed—like you were part of something bigger than yourself, and all your problems shrank in comparison to the power of the universe at work. Maybe the feeling lasted only a heartbeat—yet, you knew it. You recognized it. It was there.

Because Love is intelligent, we can ask it to teach us. In its spiritual essence, Love is a portal, a pathway, a compass, and a barometer. It is both an overarching strategy and a tool to realize our most expansive potential.

When you move into the Soul View of Love and summon the intention to lead with love regardless of the situation, love will move and fill every opening. It will teach you the way—maybe through the whispers of Heart, more expansive narratives in Mind, or the deep, grounded knowing of Body. This Love will always feel good. It will be sometimes subtle, sometimes loud and clever, sometimes even a little uncertain— yet it will always be resonant.

No matter what your journey has been, or what your current 911 looks like, you are worthy of this expansive love. Right now. This minute. Every minute. Because Love never had to do with worthiness.

Settle into the purity of the love you are, and allow yourself to be held in the arms of Love, of life, of All That Is.

That's the secret—the key that unlocks every door.

On a Soul level, you already know that you are Love. It's the fully human part of you that gets a bit lost. The whirl of Mind perceptions, the judgments of the world, the thousands of messages that whisper, "You're not really enough": these are everywhere. But consider this: what if you didn't have to perfect your whole life to #Instagram standards to relax into the Love you are? What if Love could just … be?

Opening to Love is reclaiming your original essence. It's a remembrance of who you were before all the perceptions, limiting beliefs, and life experiences got in the way. When you enter this holy reassembly, you return to the I AM essence of your truest nature.

Speak it now.

- I AM confidence.
- I AM powerful.
- I AM abundant.
- I AM LOVE.

Regardless of the I AM you desire, Love is the gateway. It always prevails, and never ends. Root in, and drench yourself in Love. Anchor in a knowing beyond form—in the wisdom of Soul, the beauty of Heart. When you come from Love in all things, what you see changes—and, if you will allow it, it will also change you.

So, how to begin?

Small acts of love are the bridge between where you are now and where you are being called. Well, actually, there is no such thing as a "small" act of love. The energetic ripple of anything done in love is beyond comprehension—because, for a moment of yours or someone else's life, love will have transmuted fear, and your Soul will *remember*.

The practices in this chapter will help you expand your birthright of Love, ignite the dream in your Heart, and contribute to the greater good in Service. Even if you are unclear on the path forward, keep Love moving in your air space through these practices. Resting in awareness, you will access deeper wisdom. Just for today, stay awake and meet each moment as your best self—your Loving self—and trust life to move and serve through you in perfect unfoldment.

You are ready.

In our journey together, you have gained wisdom about who you really are in the context of this Earth School adventure. I'm confident that you've received illumination around the messages contained in your 911; from this point forward, you will continue to gain clarity around the invitation from your Soul and what Soul is asking you to become. Deeper truths have been revealed, and will continue to reveal themselves through your openness and willingness to explore new avenues in life.

(And if you're wondering, "Was something actually revealed?" I offer this: love can't help but reveal itself when you've made the invitation. Keep noticing what you notice. Be still. Listen. It will become clearer if it's not already.)

What has emerged—or is about to emerge—is what you hold as sacred. Your sacred "Yes!" Those ever-more-vivid dreams of yours. With Soul's never-ending belief and encouragement, you can eradicate denial and self-repression, and choose freedom and congruence instead.

Now, more than ever, you are ready to reimagine what your life could be. You, on fire, fully alive, living free in joy: this is what is waiting for you, and what you know within is not only possible, it's *meant* for you. Through Love, you are empowered to re-author your story, and see how life has been in service to you, and to your Soul's miraculous vision, all along.

THE BEAUTY OF THE "AND"

When you say yes to love, you move into harmony with yourself and the flow of life. That flow—as we've discussed all along—can sometimes be delicious and beautiful and wonderful, and at other times gutting and challenging. Yet, it is all in service of your remembrance. You are Soul with a body, and above all, you are Love.

Saying yes to Love isn't about conjuring easy, pretty, storybook love. It's about embracing your own evolution— and allowing both steady, pure Spiritual Love and exciting, dynamic emotional love to be part of the holistic journey.

The most effective way I've found to live in Love in a grounded, tangible way is to embrace all seven of The Soul Solution principles to the highest degree possible. In each, you are invited to return to Love, and to the truth of who you are.

Love's intelligence will show you how to speak, what to think, and what next right action to take. Love will guide you and teach you. It will give you eagle eyes and access to expansive vision, as well as humility and the hands-on blessing of visible Earth helpers. Sometimes, Love is a miraculous shift in mindset and perception; at others, it's being doused with a cold bucket full of grace.

Most of all, Love—as it exists in the beauty of the "and"— is forgiveness.

Through forgiveness, you are empowered to give yourself what you most yearn for: unconditional love, support, and acknowledgment (and make no mistake: forgiveness is for *you*). If you struggle with seeing yourself as whole, lovable, worthy, or beautiful, ask Love to help you see yourself through its eyes, and forgive yourself for those times when you hurt yourself in its pursuit. Curiosity, compassion, tenderness, grace; these are jewels to anchor yourself in the truth of the Love that is you.

Love invites you to love those things about yourself you deem unlovable, and forgive yourself for that misperception. In the practice section, you'll get a chance to unpack this in more depth. I'll bet that once you really discern what is sitting underneath the traits, choices, or behaviors you find unlovable, you will find a path toward something you truly desire. We humans tend to default to lashing out or lashing in—anchoring in less productive emotions and wounding ourselves and others—when all along we just wanted Love.

Don't worry if you don't nail all of this on the first try. Love will give you countless chances.

Working *with* Love

You say yes to Love by living as the Soul you are—the most expanded, wise, loving, and aligned you. As a Soul, you are all of the knowledge, wisdom, love, and power, within and beyond. The universe is available for your summoning.

You are not a human with a soul. You are Soul having a human experience.

So, it's probably no surprise that the daily practice of living in Love is best expressed through The Soul Solution—the principles we have learned together in this book.

> **I align with my Soul to discover my truth**
>
> **I direct my Mind in service of my Soul**
>
> **I honor my Body as the vehicle of my Soul**
>
> **I tune into my Heart to illuminate the way**
>
> **I generate Gratitude for all that was, is, and will be**
>
> **I live in Service to life, and life is in service to me**
>
> **I am Love and say yes to leading with love**

As a Soul, you discover your truth through remembering. Your 911s are always in service to that remembering, because Soul is always calling you home to yourself.

Along the path, storms will occur—internally or externally. Mind will support you in solving problems through the lens of Love and higher potentiality. With the expansive Mind at your disposal, you can direct, reimagine, and activate your creator energy with utter brilliance. What you imagine, you can create—or, life and Soul will step in with something even better that is meant for you. Holy wow.

When you honor your Body, you honor the desires that yearn to be realized through you. This sacred vessel is your vehicle for grand travels, both within and without. It is a container of wisdom, wonder, and awe. Treasure what it is, and what it is not.

Your Heart is the symphony conductor, guiding Mind and Body in harmony through Soul's will and knowing. In your heart space, you are reminded that you are whole, not broken. The voice of Soul is amplified in the chambers of the Heart; there, you will be inspired, held, and guided forward. Invite the light to further illume your light; when you do, your very presence will be an expression of Love.

Gratitude is daily sustenance—an automatic energy amplified that moves you into vibrational alignment with your desires and your highest good. It serves as a lighthouse to help you understand and navigate the range of emotions inherent to life as a human. With Gratitude, you can decode and find a generative meaning in any event, up to and including your loudest 911s.

Every moment of every day, life is serving you. When you consciously choose to serve life in return, you embody the truth of Service as an aligned expression of Love.

Love: the unbounded expansiveness of you. Love led you to this work, and love will be your light through any 911. Something is growing inside you: a knowing that you are a co-creator capable of living as the greatest possibility of Soul's perfection. Live your truths as love. Be bright. You are leading others home to themselves.

Nature *and* Love

Nature taught me how to rest in the intelligence of Love.

There is love in every natural unfolding. Rather than competition and selection, Nature is a model of cooperation. When I stop, watch, and listen, I see cosmic love in every interaction of plants, animals, rivers, oceans, land, and sky. There is no judgment, no repression. Every part of the natural world shows up daily to give its life force in service to the whole. Each plays a role as an expression of Love. Each shows us how to transmute fear to peace.

Nature is a living, breathing incarnation of Spiritual Love. It can't do anything but embrace its fullness—and so, it teaches us to embrace our own. Nature doesn't care in the same way we humans think of caring; it's just present, and by being present, it invites you into that same freedom. When I am barefoot, grounded in the natural electricity of the Earth, Love's vibration enters my being. A sense of harmony and balance return. The sights and sounds pour Love over my physical being, soaking into my skin and Heart. Nature whispers, sometimes gently, sometimes with wild abandon, "Beloved, you are Love."

Practices

As with prior practices, it's important to engage with these exercises from the depth of your Spiritual Heart, rather than from the analysis of Mind. You know the way. Get grounded. Empty your mind. Connect sky to earth. Drop into your deep, wise Heart center, and listen.

Ask Love

Invite Love to lead the way by asking these key questions:

- "What would Love say?"
- "What would Love do?"
- "How would Love like to use me in this moment?"
- "Will this choice be life-illuminating or life-draining?"

I AM

What is the I AM energy you desire to be and experience?

- I AM_____
- I AM_____
- I AM_____

Love's Unbounded Potential

Often, we constrain our imagination. We don't want to look or feel or sound stupid. This practice may feel silly, yet it is so powerful.

- Identify something you would like to experience, or a solution you would like to create. No limits here, only possibility. Go bigger than realistically possible.

- Put upbeat, inspiring music on. Stand up and move to the music. Move those arms and legs; no one is watching! Speak your desires and dreams out loud as you move. Allow the words to pour through. However they come out, it's all good. New words and visions will begin to flow through in vivid detail as you get out of your head and into your Body.

- Imagine the answers, pathways, and resources you have requested being formed in the universal field. Let them travel on rays of sunlight back into your being.

- As you complete your waking dream, rest in silence. Let possibility take root in your blood and bones. Let it reverberate through your whole cellular system as you feel and know—it's alive. Done. Realized.

- End with a "Thank you!" to your Soul, and to the universe. Offer your trust to the great mystery of life, and know that whatever is meant to be realized through you will be.

- Come back to this playground often. The more you do it, the more fun and powerful it gets!

Loving the Unlovable

This practice is an invitation to expand the Love you have for yourself, and practice forgiveness.

- Create a comfortable setting for yourself. Light a candle, snuggle under a blanket, grab your favorite beverage, and settle in.

- Make a list of all the reasons you do not love yourself. It can be anything at all—a trait (like impatience, a hot temper, etc.), a health condition, a relationship status, finances, a choice you made that you now regret.

- One by one, take the things you haven't loved about yourself, and get curious about what lies underneath each thing. For example, if you wrote, "I don't love that I'm impatient," ask your Spiritual Heart what fuels the impatience. Chances are, you'll hear something like, "I get impatient because I worry that if a project gets sidetracked, I'll be judged by my boss." Or, maybe it's, "I get impatient with my children because all I want for them is a better life and I worry their behaviors will hinder them." Or, "I am always exhausted after a long day at work, and I get short with my answers."

- Consider what you've learned about yourself. When you really listen to what is informing your choices or behaviors, you'll recognize that these things are worthy of compassion, not disdain. More, you will start to feel seen, heard, valued, appreciated, and acknowledged.

- The part of you which you are judging is seeking love. What would this part of you ask from Love?

- Revisit your list. Apply Love-based words and actions. Lead with compassion for the part of you that sought love, even if it wasn't in the best or most aligned way.

- With expanded grace and love of self, take these wisdom bits into your day. When you encounter messy moments, practice seeing beyond your words and actions. You will notice that you move through your day with more Love, compassion, and self-care.

- With practice, you can also apply this work to others. What might they need or want from Love? Beneath their challenging actions, what parts of them are wanting to be seen, heard, or loved?

Forgiveness Practice

You are empowered to give yourself what you most long to hear and receive.

This is very different than denying a difficult or painful experience. The invitation is toward another layer of liberation, not to excuse harm that was done or is being done.

This exercise is particularly helpful if you are wanting or hoping that someone in your life will finally give you the Love you long for. This practice invites you to accept (or open to acceptance) that it may not happen through them; they may never offer what you desire. The waiting and hoping is keeping you held captive or playing small. You can give to yourself what you desire, and free yourself from the bonds of conditional, emotional love.

Step 1: Bring alive the words you've always wanted to hear, and offer them to yourself.

Create a quiet, comfortable space. Enter into stillness. Intend to be with what arises from your deeper wisdom. With each of the following questions, ground, empty, connect, breathe, and listen.

- What arises when you tune into forgiveness?
- What words are you wanting or wishing to hear?
- What actions are you wanting or wishing to receive?

Out loud, or through conscious action, offer yourself what you desire to hear and receive. Feel the words and actions. Wrap yourself in unconditional Love.

Step 2: Tune into something or someone you want to forgive.

- Open the space for the possibility of forgiveness with yourself or someone else. Remember, this is a choice to liberate yourself in Spiritual Love, and move through and beyond the pain of conditional love. If you are not yet ready to forgive yourself or the person involved, honor that; instead, intend or ask for willingness to see this situation with the eyes of your Soul. Say, "I am open to seeing this differently."

- Tune in and ask Love about forgiveness. What would Love like me to know? How does Love see this? What would Love say? How would Love move through this? How would Love thrive beyond this?

- If you have wronged yourself or someone else, take ownership of the act. If possible, apologize in person, tuning into Love before the conversation. If that's not possible (or if you prefer not to), imagine energetically speaking to yourself or the other person as your higher self. Or, simply surrender the situation to your Soul or the higher power of your understanding. Play with all the ways you can forgive, offer Love, and raise the vibration of the relationship or situation.

Living *in* Love

Love is within you, around you, above you, below you, to the left and to the right. Summon it. It will unfailingly respond, for it was never gone.

May the depth and sagacity that Love is be your embodied presence, guide, and teacher. Love wants you to know that this is who you are. Always whole, without question or doubt. Love is you, and you are love.

For Mary, the greatest challenge was remembering that she was Love all along. This knowledge was buried under all of her past experiences and false beliefs that she was not enough. As a result, love felt elusive to her emotional Heart, and her mind was mired in fear.

She now considers her ex-husband to be one of her greatest teachers in life. He couldn't give her what she needed, yet he was ultimately the catalyst for her reclaiming the Love she was seeking all along. When she learned to hear the voice of Love, and insisted (in the best way) that Love lead the way in her life, Love became her mission and purpose.

Mary's willingness to embrace Love brought her from a compartmentalized life to living in harmony. She now knows that Love is the nature of all that she is.

"I'd call it a miracle," Mary says now. "And that miracle is ... *me*."

Love is, always has been, and always will be, our one shared purpose.

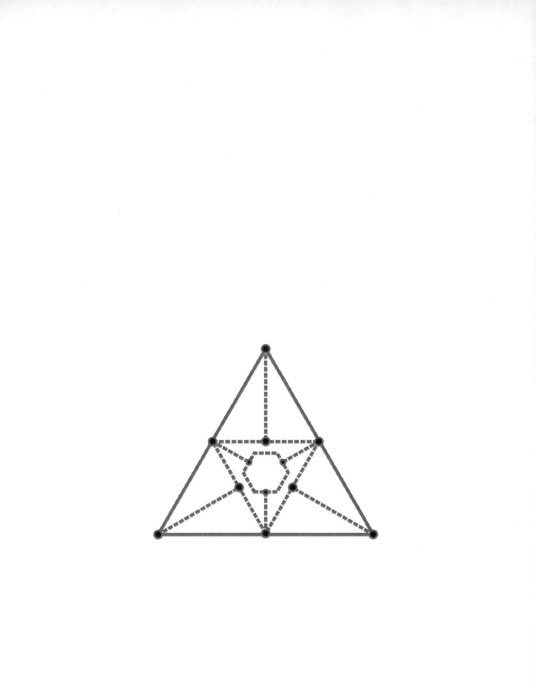

Part III

The Expansion

Imagine.

Nearly 8 billion lights

consciously choosing to enliven the power of Love.

All is possible.

Holy wow.

Chapter 11

Living EnSouled

In my perfect, spiritually-informed life, I arise early to meditate. I fuel my body with healthy, organic foods, and my mind with empowered vision and thoughts. I sit in stillness for long periods of time and tune into powerful wisdom and expanded intelligence that makes the day—and my future—even better than I imagined. I set the intention to choose joy and move through the day perfectly calm and centered, feeling limitless and empowered by love. I skillfully surf the waves of life, whether calm or chaotic, with ease and grace. I always treat others with the care of unconditional love. I manifest everything I want, and life is always easy and joyful. I offer life-changing services that empower my clients to realize outcomes about which they are beyond ecstatic. I give generously and make a meaningful impact and contribution to humanity. I am fully alive, fully in love with life, prosperous, and certain I am making a difference …

"Hold on, Thomps," I hear you saying. "Is that really how you live? And, more importantly, is that how you expect me to live when I finish this book?"

Well … not quite.

I *do* get up early to meditate. I *do* love my life. I *do* feel like I can surf life's waves with more ease than I did years ago, and I certainly feel like my life is more meaningful, and on-purpose than it was when I lived without these spiritual principles.

Am I constantly dancing around on a cloud of bliss, stress and challenge free?

Some days, absolutely.

Other days, not a chance.

I think the messages that life is supposed to be constantly joyful, blissful, and easy are a form of spiritual misinformation. After so much hard work, we reason, we're supposed to get a reward—like "reaching enlightenment," or "leaving our human ego behind." Yes, every experience in life is possible, because you are a limitless Soul having a human journey. Yet, we came here for Earth School. Our growth is influenced by how we meet and make meaning of the ups and downs of life. It depends on us embracing the parts of us that are fully human, and integrating them with the infinite wisdom that is our Soul. It means living, in all ways, in the beauty of the "and."

The interior journey, which is initiated and enlivened by the Seven Principles explored in this book, reflects to us not the imagined perfection of our human desires, but the perfection of Nature. There will be, in life, a dynamic exchange and balance. There will be seasons of change. There will be times of great beauty, abundance, and ease—and there will be times of chaos when renewal and restoration seem unlikely, or even impossible.

Life is never going to be seventy-five degrees and sunny every day—not even in Southern California. We are in Earth School to learn, grow, and evolve. It won't look or feel perfect every day—yet it will *be* perfect, because your Soul knows the path, and life is always moving in service to you.

You are more powerful than you can imagine. You do have a say in creating the life and impact you desire. The more you engage with the principles and practices in this book, the more you will step into the space of limitlessness and love that you are.

Yet to imagine that you'll one day land at *the* destination— that, someday, you'll finally arrive and never have to experience a challenge again ... that is not the purpose of your 911, or where life is leading you. You are being called to move, live, and thrive in ever-expanding ways, and with each new experience you will discover new ways to connect with and come home to your Soul.

Taking YOU *to the* World

Every thought, feeling, breath, and action matter. All you do, and all you are, ripples out for a broader impact and collective experience.

When you are aware of this, you begin to live it. You see all the places where you are woven into the fabric of life. It's incredible. And once you see the interconnectedness of your life to all life, you will never unsee it.

Above all else in life, you get to be you, and do you. Whatever your desires are, you can experience and contribute to life as the fully empowered I AM version of you, in all your glory. You are a billion shades of beautiful expression—love sharing love, in service to your life, and all of life. You can choose to have the kind of life you've always wanted to experience, while extending an invitation to others to do the same.

Living as Soul, in alignment with Love, you are empowered to re-author your story—the next chapter, and the whole arc of your life. Fire up that imagination of yours, and make it the most incredible, miraculous version you can envision. Soul knows what this expanded capacity and capability is for you, and how you can bring your superhuman qualities to all that you do, no matter where or how you're doing it.

Sometimes, embracing the message of your 911 and the invitation back to Soul means doing something more or different. Other times, it means dialing it back and learning how to *be* without all the doing. Before all periods of great growth is that time in the seed, under the ground, taking nourishment while listening and growing and preparing. Honor where you are in your process. This alone is a tremendous gift.

Above all, let the seven principles of The Soul Solution guide and inform you along whatever path Soul leads you down.

The practices in this book are not just intended to help you move through your 911 and into the learning and life that awaits you on the other side. They are intended to expand your awareness of your interconnections with all of life, and empower you to live that interconnectedness deliberately, every day.

So, experiment and explore. What practices are you willing to commit to engaging with on a daily basis? What practices felt resonant and led to a meaningful insight or experience? What still feels like a stretch, yet you are willing to give it a sincere effort? As you ponder these questions, ask Soul and Heart. Your answers and guidance will be different than if you lead with Mind in isolation. Importantly, listen to Body for resonance, adapt the practices, and make them your own.

Bringing Soul *To* Work

I view business as the largest breathing organism alive, and the largest change agent in the world. There is no one and no thing (people, plants, animals, land, sky, and everything in between) that business does not touch, serve, or impact.

No matter how you engage with business in your life—whether you own a business, work for a business, or buy from businesses—you are part of a business ecosystem. And, just like one organism in a natural ecosystem can support or derail an entire food chain, every person in the ecosystem of business is a potential force with the power to change the very nature of business. Whether in small, ordinary ways, or momentous ones, you have the power to sway the impact of business on the collective simply by hearing and growing through your 911, responding via all seven of The Soul Solution principles in this book, and showing up as a new, Soul-connected version of you.

In this evolutionary time, there is a magnitude of opportunity never seen before. Business, by its systemic nature and impact across the planet (and beyond), is poised to become the most pivotal force for good in our world—*if* we choose to define its nature as such.

Given that some forms of business are currently among the most destructive forces in our world, that feels like a big "if." However, the shift isn't as difficult, or as far away, as it might seem from an Earth View perspective. When Soul and Love are leading, no problem is too big to solve. There are no impossibilities, and no exclusions.

As the recipient of a 911 from your Soul, your mission (should you choose to accept it), is to be a force for change within the living, breathing organism of your workplace. Within a 911 is a growth invitation you can pay forward every day, in key moments; there is always someone who can benefit from you, your learnings and evolution.

I know, that sounds big. It sounds bold. It sounds aspirational, even revolutionary.

It may also sound like a lot of work.

And yet, it's often not the big gestures that will create transformation within your workplace. It's simply *you*, showing up every day and making small, tangible choices directed by and empowered by Soul.

I work with many high-level leaders across diverse ecosystems. Although it's a small sample relative to the global database, I suspect that my clients are a good representation of leadership as a whole. The majority report similar experiences in their work lives: back-to-back meetings (which means that actual work time falls outside of normal business hours), little time to rise above reactivity, and constant pressure to deliver more with less. While the metrics may differ from industry to industry, the expectation is the same: get the job done, whatever it takes. When that expectation is in place, it can come at a tremendous cost to your health, family, joy, or well-being.

I often hear the phrase, "I sold my soul to this career."

If that's how you are feeling, this awareness can be an invaluable turning point for you. The time for change is *now*. You have the wisdom and power to reclaim life and living in a way that is aligned with the highest expression of you. The biggest gaps are visible when you reflect upon what you wished you could be doing if you had more time. Connect with Soul, for it will surely reveal the pathway to greater aliveness and harmony.

Although no company would ever give voice to sentiments like, "You must deliver at all costs," or, "Be willing to sacrifice your life for this job" in their role description, the unspoken message is clear nonetheless. There is a cost to hit targets, and leaders should pay it readily, or someone else will. This may sound harsh—however, even if its unintended, this is the kind of pressure many leaders feel.

The leaders I work with are incredibly dedicated. It's amazing how much they juggle, both personally and professionally.

They are committed to growing their knowledge, leadership, and skill sets constantly; whatever best practices, leading-edge tools, or new strategies are available, they're on it. And if it's not available they create it. Because of this dedication, they and their teams contribute in extraordinary ways to business success year after year.

However, because the demands of leadership require them to move fast, make tough decisions quickly, and think on their feet, there is little room for tapping into the quantum-level genius of Soul or accessing the intelligence available beyond the five senses.

Life doesn't just speak to you with regard to your personal Soul, purpose, and experiences. It also speaks to you about the dynamic potential of the collective, and how you can live and lead from the inflection point of the "and" as a fully-connected being with access to your own highest potential.

This is a powerful invitation to ask your Spiritual Heart: "What is being left on the table because I haven't made room for Soul in business?" New ways of being that create the cultural experience you crave for? New innovations? New partnerships? New policies? A broader mission that is conscious of the bigger impact on the environment, community, or globe?

I wonder what wants to come alive in you and through you? Never underestimate the power of what lies inside.

Regardless of what your work looks like, what industry you're in, whether you're in a traditional leadership role or leading as an innovator in some other way, you have the chance to view your work as more than just a means to an end. Your job, no matter what it is, is an assignment from Soul—or, rather, it's a collection of assignments through which you are called to serve your growth, and the growth of those around you.

As with all of life, there's something bigger going on here. Create stillness, get quiet, tune into your Heart, and ask, "What is my *real* work here?"

THE NEXT STRATEGIC DISRUPTORS

Soul and Love are the next strategic disruptors for business— and the way they unfold is through you.

You are part of a grander plan and an element of the creative force that is shaping the whole. Every time you align with the highest potential of your true nature, every time you get deeply present, every time you recognize your impact on those around you, you are taking a stand for positive change.

A leader grounded in Soul and Love is aware of their own energy, mindful of how they speak, and are receptive to and take responsibility for the systemic impact of their choices on people and the planet. They actively choose their mindset, get curious about dismantling old paradigms and procedures, and welcome the unfamiliar. They are conscious, awake, and aligned to a bigger mission, and to the role they are here to play within that mission—and they know, right down to their bones, that *this is bigger than them.* They deeply value each individual and know all have a vital role to play.

In order to step up and meet this challenge, they rely on more than intellect alone. They trust their instincts, and listen to how life is speaking to, around, and through them. They create time to connect to the well of wisdom within, knowing it will help them make better choices about people, money, resources, procedures, and products. They hold fewer meetings to free up capacity, and encourage their employees to tap into their expanded potentiality and bring that wisdom back to the team. They are willing to experiment with new team practices to catalyze the exponential intelligence of the whole (visible and invisible). One such practice is offered below and can be adapted beyond individual use to group application.

When things do go off the rails, these leaders lead by example. They enter stillness to discern the best path forward, and align their actions accordingly. They've learned that taking a break ignites creative solutioning that is not available when they are under great pressure. When temporary emotions of fear or anxiety arise, they pause, garner the insights these energies offer, and engage in productive outlets for release.

Most of all, they won't tolerate "selling their soul" for a pair of golden handcuffs or fear of perceived loss. They take a stand for their health, relationships, joy, community, and beyond. They are committed to delivering with excellence, yet are no longer willing to compromise the quality of their life. They own their true nature as ensouled beings, and even when others question or judge, they hold steady in their highest self, and trust their knowing that life is speaking through them.

There are also realities in business. It is always the "and." Profits, imperatives, and expectations are crucial; without financial viability, a company can't do its work as a functional ecosystem. As a leader, you can't just sit around and meditate all day. Still, you can choose to give yourself the time and space to connect with your Soul, Heart, and Body every day, and bring forth that deeper wisdom and alignment in your presence and approach to daily objectives. You can seize every opportunity to claim your inner brilliance and encourage your team to claim theirs. Working in this way will empower everyone to serve with more joy, offer unconventional solutions, and feel confident, safe, and supported.

Imagine a company where every employee felt fully alive, inspired, and lived into their highest potentiality ... a collective body of unlimited potential and possibility in service of the greater good. Holy wow.

Nature *and* Your Soul Work

Some of my favorite places to visit are the redwood forests along the Northern Californian coast.

I have experienced some of my most powerful interior connections while sitting amongst the redwoods. Words cannot even begin to capture what being in the arms of a redwood forest feels like in my body.

Most of all, I am struck by the redwoods' intertwined root systems. These trees literally support one another during storms, and provide daily protection and nutrients to other forest inhabitants. The secret to their great vitality and remarkable longevity is their life-enhancing collaborative network.

The redwoods teach us to work together. To hold each other

up. To feed and nourish and provide a place of safe haven for one another. They have seen and heard and lived through so much—and, when we practice listening with Soul and Heart, we too can learn from their wisdom for strength, love, guidance, and perspective.

Practices

A Roundtable with the Masters

A wonderful way to enliven greater potentiality available to you is to invite a team of mentors and great messengers to engage in an "ideation consultation."

There's one caveat: they don't have to be alive.

In your imagination, see yourself seated around a table with anyone and everyone you'd like to learn from, living or not. Tell them what you are up to. Ask questions. You can even imagine a dialogue taking place around you. Then, breathe deeply and listen.

The answers you seek might come to you right away, or later in the week (or month). At some point, however, you will be surprised by new knowledge, insight, direction, or connection.

Access to greater possibility—awakened!

A Final Note *on* Living as Soul

If you've ever wondered, *Do I matter? Do I really make a difference?* the answer is unequivocally, "Yes!"

I don't have to know you personally to know this truth. You matter deeply. Every single day, you are already making a difference. You really are that powerful.

Most of us have lost sight of who we are—a Soul, enlivened—and how much we can and do influence our life and the lives of others. The most delicious part is that, now, you get to choose again. How would you like to consciously shape the experience of your own life, others' lives, and life itself, in business and at home? Imagine what you could be a catalyst to creating!

Holy wow.

What you crave and long for, others long for too.

The answers are about twelve inches away—the length of one intentional shift from your mind to your Spiritual Heart. There lies a treasure trove of jewels and gifts beyond imagination. Soul you—the true you, who you've been longing to meet again—is there. Life and business, as a collection of Souls, seeks this very return as well.

With Soul and Love, all is possible. It is already who you are. It is already who we are.

Breathe. Drink this in. Let it saturate every cell in your being. Then …

Onward.

As Soul, and as Love.

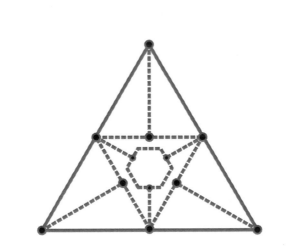

A Love Note *from* Soul

Dear One,

Rest in the infinite knowing

of the I AM presence you are.

Be certain.

That all you need.

That all you seek.

That all you long for.

Is available.

You are guided.

You are protected.

You are loved.

Forever and always, I cherish you.

I love you unconditionally.

I am your answer to a life fulfilled.

So, tune in.

I'll light the way.

Forever and always loving You!

With love,

Your Soul

Resources

Join Jeanine's Community

Website: www.JeanineThompson.net
Instagram: @_jeaninethompson_
LinkedIn: www.LinkedIn.com/in jeanine-thompson-61089611
Facebook: www.Facebook.com/jeaninethompsonllc

Book Jeanine to Speak

Visit www.JeanineThompson.net/speaking

Discover Jeanine's Potentiality Coaching

Explore Immersive coaching and leadership assessments at
www.JeanineThompson.net/work-with-me

Jeanine's Book Resources, Events, & Nature Pictures

www.JeanineThompson.net/author

Additional Resources to Support Living Your Highest Expression.

Each of these providers offer a plethora of free resources and services to invest in, via their websites and social media channels. Happy exploring! *Note, I am not a paid affiliate of any resources offered. Rather, those included, I've personally received great benefit from.*

Advancing Leadership and High Performance
www.HighPerformanceInstitute.com

Emotional Freedom Tapping (EFT)
www.TheTappingSolution.com

HeartMath Institute
www.HeartMath.org

Numerologist/performance consultant/hypnotherapist
www.SaraJessicaLaamanen.com

Intuitive bodywork/energy practitioner
www.EmilyHallListening.com

Acknowledgments

As I sat down to capture my gratitude to all who have influenced the creation of *911 from your Soul*, I was in awe of the vast support, love, and wisdom I've been blessed to receive. My heart is bursting with joy, gratitude, and love.

Thank you to my family. To my children, Tanner and Taylor, it has been an honor and privilege to be your mom. Thank you for your love and support always, and especially through the development of this book.

To my mom and dad (loving me from beyond), thank you for life. It is because of the love you once shared that I get to traverse this beautiful playground of Earth School. Thank you for being my first teachers and for loving me as you do.

To my sister Janae and her husband Kevin, I am so grateful

for your generous support, tons of giggles and love of me and my children.

A special thank you to my Grandma Marion (loving me from beyond) and my Aunt Judi who role model unconditional love. To all my family - big love and gratitude to each of you.

Thank you to Bryna Haynes, my editor and publisher, and founder of WorldChangers Media. Holy wow! I am in awe of your strategic vision, ability to tune into an author's essence, and genius in helping create powerful, mission-oriented books that can change lives. You are an Earth Angel, treasured gift, and blessing to partner with. Love you, and deep bow. And thank you to your brilliant team for creating a quality experience for the readers.

Thank you to Marci Shimoff, I am forever grateful for divine synchronicity and the immeasurable gift of you. The genesis of this work was birthed during your mentorship and invaluable wisdom, support, and love. You are the most generous person I know, and I'm deeply blessed to have you in my life. Love you, and deep bow.

Thank you to the vast, wise teachers (both living and those before me). Through each phase of growth, the perfect teachers appeared in divine timing and were instrumental to each iteration of who I am and am becoming. Namaste.

Thank you to my teams, past and present. You are invaluable teachers and partners. Serving with excellence and success are made possible because of the wisdom and diversity of your collective talents. Big gratitude and love.

Thank you to my cherished circle of friends. Sandy, our

friendship began 52 years ago, and each year is more wonderous. My core high school friends, thank you for 4 decades of the privilege of laughing until we cry and holding each other through life's fullness. To my college friends, deep bow, the love you are adds crazy big joy to my life. Thank you to the treasured friends that arrived and accompanied me along progressive passages of life post college. You make life rich, joyful, and rewarding. As individuals and a collective tribe, you have played a vital role in my Soul's journey and showered me with love beyond measure. Thank you for walking with me on this grand adventure. With big love and gratitude.

Thank you to the Earth angels who have been endlessly supportive throughout the development of this book: Sara, Michelle, Emily, Lisa, Naomi, Lisa, Lesley, Renita, Susan, and Ginny. Cosmic-sized love and appreciation.

Thank you to my clients. I learn from you every day and am exceedingly grateful for the privilege of knowing and being in service to you as you live your highest potentiality.

Thank you to Shari and Alex of Shari Fleming Photography for the gorgeous front cover image. It was a day of light and joy on stunning land. I love beauty and the two of you are exceptionally gifted at capturing life's precious moments in all its radiant brilliance.

Thank you to the invisible realm, to God and the host of celestial helpers guiding me and all expressions of life to realize all we came here to be. Thank you for infinite love, guidance, and support.

Thank you to the Forest and the lands where I write. You

are my muse, a vital life force and a feast of awe and wonder igniting unbounded love.

A final thank you, to my readers. May this offering of love wrap its arms around you and ignite within a remembrance of who you are, and how much you are loved.

One Tree Planted is a 501(c)(3) nonprofit dedicated to global reforestation. They plant trees to restore nature and biodiversity. They also raise awareness about the importance of trees, offer businesses like ours a simple sustainability solution, and motivate younger generations to do something positive for the environment.

For every copy purchased, one tree will be planted.

About *the* Author

Jeanine Thompson's breadth of knowledge and experience spans multiple disciplines and professional expressions, from clinical psychotherapy to global business to spiritual growth. At the core of her diverse career is a passionate dedication to helping individuals live their highest potentiality.

As a highly successful, former Fortune 50 executive, she led diverse human resource teams across the globe, delivered keynotes to large audiences, and helped navigate the way toward profitability while empowering personal and professional growth. An agent of change, she was a key leader supporting complex global acquisitions and divestitures.

For nearly a decade, Jeanine led a thriving evidence-based psychotherapy practice treating the range of anxiety disorders. She was honored to guide her clients' transformations and heightened levels of well-being, joy, and harmony. A Reiki Master and former certified yoga instructor, she has a deep reverence for the power of energy and the body's innate wisdom.

She also holds a Master of Social Work (MSW) and numerous certifications including Certified High Performance Coach (CHPC) and Rapid Transformational Therapy Practitioner (RTTP). Jeanine was personally mentored by renowned transformational expert Marci Shimoff, and trains yearly with the High Performance Institute, founded by Brendon Burchard. She is insatiably curious and loves to engage in immersive studies on vast perspectives to advance personal and business mastery.

As a potentiality coach, speaker, and author, Jeanine now partners with individuals, teams, and audiences in service of living all you came here to be and elevating the highest good of humanity.

Committed to service and sustainability, Jeanine has volunteered for decades with hospice clients and their families as they step through life's journey and transitions. She cares deeply about the planet and creating a business that gives back to nature, and is thrilled to partner with One Tree Planted to plant one tree for every book sold.

About the Publisher

Founded in 2021 by Bryna Haynes, WorldChangers Media is a boutique publishing company focused on "Ideas for Impact." We know that great books change lives, topple outdated paradigms, and build movements. Our commitment is to deliver superior-quality transformational nonfiction by, and for, the next generation of thought leaders.

Ready to write and publish your thought leadership book with us? Learn more at www.WorldChangers.Media.

Made in United States
North Haven, CT
29 June 2023

38283492R00181